REDEMPTIVE CRIMINOLOGY

New Horizons in Criminology series

Series Editor: **Andrew Millie**, Edge Hill University, UK

New Horizons in Criminology provides concise, authoritative texts which reflect cutting-edge thought and theoretical development with an international scope. Written by leading authors in their fields, the series has become essential reading for all academics and students interested in where criminology is heading.

Coming soon in paperback:

Transnational Criminology
Simon Mackenzie

Out now in the series:

Visual Criminology
Bill McClanahan

A Criminology Of Narrative Fiction
Rafe McGregor

Transnational Criminology
Simon Mackenzie

Wildlife Criminology
Angus Nurse and **Tanya Wyatt**

Find out more at
bristoluniversitypress.co.uk/new-horizons-in-criminology

NEW HORIZONS IN CRIMINOLOGY

REDEMPTIVE CRIMINOLOGY

Aaron Pycroft and Clemens Bartollas

BRISTOL
UNIVERSITY
PRESS

First published in Great Britain in 2022 by

Bristol University Press
University of Bristol
1-9 Old Park Hill
Bristol
BS2 8BB
UK
t: +44 (0)117 374 6645
e: bup-info@bristol.ac.uk

Details of international sales and distribution partners are available at bristoluniversitypress.co.uk

British Library Cataloguing in Publication Data
A catalogue record for this book is available from the British Library

ISBN 978-1-5292-0353-0 hardcover
ISBN 978-1-5292-0354-7 ePub
ISBN 978-1-5292-0352-3 ePdf

Cover design: Bristol University Press
Front cover image: Shutterstock/Rudolf Otrokov
Bristol University Press use environmentally responsible print partners.
Printed and bound in Great Britain by CPI Group (UK) Ltd,
Croydon, CR0 4YY

For our grandchildren with love

From Aaron to Willow Grace

And from Clemens to Irie, Jake, Jordan,
Rayne, Starley, Eli, Lincoln and Khosi

Contents

Acknowledgements

We are grateful to colleagues who have engaged with us in the various ways that have led to the development of this book. Particular thanks go to Glenn Jordan who sadly died in 2020. Glenn worked for the Corrymeela Community, one of the earliest peacemaking communities in Northern Ireland, where he was Programme Manager for Public Theology (https://www.corrymeela.org/news/184/remembering-glenn-jordan). We are indebted to him for highlighting the story of Ruth and its implications for peacemaking. Thanks also go to Antoni Mikulski for allowing his story to be shared and to Professor Julian Wolfreys for his expertise on the work of Derrida. Some of this work is based around other publications and we are grateful to the *Journal of Critical Criminology* for allowing us to reproduce substantial parts of Pycroft and Bartollas (2018); thanks also to the *Journal of Theoretical and Philosophical Criminology* for allowing us to use Pycroft (2018) and to Andrew Millie for allowing us to use Pycroft (2021). For Chapter 7 we are indebted to the following academic colleagues at Portsmouth, who are former probation officers, for conversations that helped to frame the discussion: Ceri Halfpenny, Laura Haggar, Michelle McDermott, Ben Keysell, Julie Eden and Jennifer Grant.

We are also grateful for the support of Professor Andrew Millie as series editor and to the Bristol University Press team who are just a delight to work with. Finally, and as ever, without the love and support of our families, especially our wives, Nicky and Linda, this book would not have happened.

Preface

This book is a narrative that has emerged from dialogue between the authors, seeking to make sense of their substantial lived experiences in criminal justice, health and welfare, and educational settings. Both are white, male academics. Aaron Pycroft is a British Roman Catholic. The Catholicism comes from Dublin via my maternal great-grandfather, whose daughter married my grandfather, a working-class communist descended from French Huguenots. My paternal side of the family, apart from being on occasion described as poachers and pirates, were wildfowlers and brick makers and low Anglicans. Clemens Bartollas is a North American Presbyterian pastor from West Virginia with extensive experience of juvenile justice, working with gangs and also serving as an expert witness in death row and murder cases. In making these differences and commonalities explicit, we are overtly seeking to embrace those differences and commonalities, and through understanding each other's perspectives, to have our own examined, challenged and maybe changed. Both authors have approached criminal justice from different directions, with varying experiences of social services and justice systems, but our conclusions are remarkably similar. Ultimately, our desire is to encourage criminal justice practitioners and students who want to be practitioners to explore the roots and horizons of their personal and collective practice. In this book we bring together perspectives in Catholicism, and its traditional emphasis on sacrifice and atonement, with Protestant understandings of grace and justification and their application to understanding processes of justice. We are seeking at least the beginning of a dialogue, centred on a concept of redemption. Underpinning our approach is an acknowledgement that as human beings we are open to our environments and criminologists who are a part of the system(s) that we study. Thus, we bring who we are to understanding the issues involved. However, we do not reduce our work to the sum total of those cultural, theological and spiritual traditions, thus these reflections form a part of our professional and personal (including confessional) journeys of discovery in the light of the texts, traditions and ideas discussed.

This is not easy work and takes us well beyond normal academic disciplines and silos. The work is deeply personal but then reflects 'the thing in itself' of justice, namely, that crime, and what we should do about it, *is* deeply personal. This is not a new insight but within the context of both the totalizing metaphysical justifications for punishment expressed in some philosophies and theologies and the breakdown of coherent thought structure in some aspects of postmodernisms we desperately need to communicate both within and across disciplines. This 'personalism' and 'individuation' goes 'all the way down', as criminologists invest (hopefully) in solutions to crime not for financial reward, or status, but to make a difference to people's lives and to help develop a just and loving society.

In 1983, aged 18, Aaron Pycroft began working as a nursing assistant in an NHS hospital for people that we then described as 'mentally handicapped', with some labelled 'spastic' due to their physical conditions. Many had been in the system for long periods of time, with their files going back to the 1950s and 1960s describing them as 'idiots', 'imbeciles' and 'insane'. A few were casualties of reacting to vaccines. Some of the much older female residents had no limitations other than having committed the misdemeanour of conceiving a child outside of marriage and were placed in institutions by their families, and other than being moved between the old Victorian hospitals, there they stayed. The dormitory ward that I worked on had about 23 beds, with boys, girls, men and women aged from about eight up to about 40 years. There was no privacy, no one bathed, dressed or fed himself or herself. The only care plan was the routine of the hospital: waking the patients, giving them a cup of tea, breakfast, baths/showers (male staff bathed and showered male and female residents), dressing, and being placed in front of the TV in an armchair for the morning. This was followed by lunch, maybe taking residents for a walk in their wheelchairs around the grounds or to the local shops in the afternoon, then tea, TV and bed.

I was fortunate to get a place at Plater College in Oxford, a Catholic institution that provided university-level education to people without formal qualifications in the heart of the Oxford University system. My contemporaries included miners, steel workers and bin men. Then in 1988, after Plater and completing an MA, I started work for Hampshire Probation Service as an assistant warden in a probation hostel with people whom we used to call 'residents'. These were predominantly young men between the ages of 18 and 25, of no fixed abode and who would be described, now, as 'prolific offenders'. Some of them worked, some were unemployed, some had alcohol, drug and mental health problems (often in combination), and most had poor literacy skills and came from what we then called 'broken homes'. The hostel provided a key worker system, some limited group work, and activities in and around the hostel such as gardening and maintenance. Each member of staff would work up to 24 hours (including sleep) in single cover shift. Service users could breach their probation orders for failure to comply with hostel rules of engaging in domestic activities, such as washing up and cleaning, and consequently be sent to prison. The focus was on getting to know people and spending a lot of time playing table tennis and pool and engaging in social activities.

In 1989 The Society of St Dismas employed me as a social worker in their housing team, providing what we then called a 'halfway house' model for street drinkers who were alcohol dependent. The Society had that year opened the first community-based Alcohol Recovery Unit (ARU) in the country, in part funded by Hampshire Probation Service and Hampshire Constabulary. Street drinkers could walk in off the street and get a detox and a period of aftercare for six weeks before moving into the 'dry housing' without the need for a prior assessment or funding agreement. By moving through the dry house and into staged accommodation and maintaining 'sobriety', the person would be offered their own council or housing association flat after about a year. I spent the next 15 years with this organization as a practitioner and eventually as the Substance Misuse Service Manager, moving into the era of the contract culture and competitive tendering.

In 2003 I then became a Senior Lecturer in Probation Studies at the Institute of Criminal Justice Studies at the University of Portsmouth, when the 'What works' agenda was in full swing as part of the team to deliver probation qualifications to different probation areas across the country. I have for the last 18 years been intimately involved in the design and delivery of these qualifications in their various iterations through trying to respond to the demands of the university, probation employers and their paymasters.

Through my research and teaching I have tried to maintain a cutting-edge perspective, but here are my key points: everything that I know about working with people who are vulnerable, experiencing difficulties and in distress, and trying to better their lives, comes from working with the lived experience of those people. Each service user that I met and worked with was an exciting opportunity for me to be challenged not to 'other the differences' between us but to acknowledge and own the difference. In sharing a 'ground of being' and by seeing myself in the face of what state and society see as the risk-presenting 'monstrous other' who is different, threatening, compulsive, out of control and criminogenic, is the basis for genuine and real communication. Buried deep in the Judaeo-Christian tradition is an understanding of the 'necessary sin of Adam' (see Chapter 6) revealing a God-given jouissance of the moment.

For Clemens Bartollas it was a strange beginning for a young boy who was constantly in trouble, seen as delinquent (perhaps even the worst kid in town), always bottom of the class, to a life in the pastoral ministry and academia. My father had died and my mother could not take care of me and I had a severe speech impediment. Only my grandfather ever had any hope that I would make something of myself. Then the summer between sophomore and junior years of high school, I had a spiritual experience and decided to become a Presbyterian minister. No one believed in me (or my spiritual experience) except my grandfather and several events took place, but I became an honours student at a Church college in West Virginia, resolved my speech impediment in a short period, and accessed academic scholarships to receive my college diploma. I have been a Professor of Criminology for the past 50 years (40 of those at the University of Northern Iowa), a

Presbyterian minister for the past 60 years, and an expert witness in death penalty cases for over 30 years.

I graduated from Princeton Theological Seminary and in my last year at Princeton, I applied for and received a job working with a white gang in the Newark, New Jersey area. My first weekend on the job I learned that my predecessor had been threatened for his life. A knife was placed on his shirt, cutting his chest a little and he was told that if he did not resign he would be killed. He resigned and I got the job! This began a process of my working with 'hard-core offenders'. I realized that I myself had grown up on the streets and was not going to be intimidated and so had no problems with those gang members that year. Neither have I had any problems of any nature in the past 50 years of working with 'hard-core' and 'violent offenders'.

I was also working as a pastor and nine years later I resigned from my church position and returned to graduate school at the Ohio State University, where I gained my PhD. I then took a job as the cottage director and social worker in a maximum-security juvenile facility for older, aggressive delinquent youth who had committed violent offences. My predecessor had an older youth jump him and nearly choked him to death but in working in this environment over the next four years, I learned that traditional treatment programmes were very ineffective. My 30 years as an expert witness in death penalty cases has allowed me, unlike many treatment agents, to approach rehabilitation through the eyes of perpetrators.

In a book I wrote on treatment early in my career (Bartollas, 1985), I made an evaluation of the rehabilitation model, originally defined as the medical model, adjustment model and reintegration model. I indicated that the medical model, which proposed offenders were sick and needed to be cured of the disease of criminality, was simply not true now if it was ever true. The adjustment model was expressed by reality therapy, transactional analysis; guided group interaction, positive peer culture, milieu therapy, the therapeutic community, and behaviour modification are based on offenders gaining in insight to correct their problems. The reintegration model assumes that offenders' problems must be solved in the community where they began. The community must offer the opportunities to develop law-abiding behaviour, and the offender must learn how to utilize these opportunities. This model seemed to have more going for it than the other two; however, it did not seem to go far enough.

In critiquing approaches to rehabilitation, I agreed that rehabilitation's assumptions conflict with basic human values and have been used to disguise the true custodial and repressive nature of correctional institutions and that the rise of the rehabilitative ideal conflicts with the values of individual liberty and volition. This book explores those cultural dynamics in some depth and explains why rehabilitative practices are designed not to work and why the practices of rehabilitation result in further punishment rather than treatment. In the name of treatment, the state has legitimized programming in offenders' lives, with fewer constraints on official services. In the name of treatment, the state has refused to release inmates until agents of the 'therapeutic state' decided they were rehabilitated, and, for difficult inmates, this resulted in prolonged terms of imprisonment resulting in a more inhumane correctional process.

In our work on complexity theory and whole systems approaches in criminal justice and social work (Pycroft and Bartollas, 2014) we identified the challenge of working and writing in a non-reductionist way. Clemens likes to say "Less is more" and I like to say, "More is more." Somewhere between these two statements (is one Catholic and one Protestant, have we flipped positions?) is hopefully the communication of superabundance and love articulated in a rereading of the Judeo-Christian understanding of redemption in the light of modern resources. In many ways, this book is a deeply personal exploration of who Clemens and I are, our friendship and understanding of each other, and our respective lived experiences. It has been a labour of love, at times painful to write, the source of disagreement, consternation and some falling out. However, it is a book about redemption; we have a feeling of celebration, and dare I say satisfaction. It is also an apt lesson in not throwing away books, keeping your books jumbled up so that you constantly come across things you weren't looking for and the importance of gifting them. I bought a 1977 copy of *Agenda* in a second-hand bookshop years ago and keep wondering why I have it, but now I know why (Chapter 7). After a visit to Iowa, Clemens loaded me down with books to come home with, including Bethge's (2000) weighty biography of Bonhoeffer, and it proved crucial to prompting our thinking when looking for inspiration. The purpose of reading is to enable us to engage with others, and through others, ourselves. Hermeneutics should challenge and provoke us to see what is really there, who the other is and who we are in the light of each other's being.

NEW HORIZONS IN CRIMINOLOGY

Professor Andrew Millie, Department of Law and Criminology, Edge Hill University, UK

Series Editor Preface

Aaron Pycroft and Clemens Bartollas have been working together for several years and have previously edited a collection on the application of complexity theory for criminal justice and social work (2014). In this new book they take complexity theory and marry it with insights from theology, philosophy, mathematics and quantum mechanics – and of course criminology – to argue for a redemptive criminology. Many criminologists take a narrow view of their subject, drawing inspiration from only sociology or social policy. But, as British criminologist David Downes once famously noted, criminology is a rendezvous subject (see Garland and Sparks, 2000) and therefore it applies knowledge and wisdom from all sorts of disciplines to the subjects of crime, harm or justice. This new book is most definitely criminology at the edge, seeking new understandings from subjects not often associated with criminology. It is a place where I often find myself with my own work, and Aaron has contributed to a recent collection that I have edited on criminology and public theology (Pycroft, 2021). Despite the social sciences often keeping their distance from religion, there is much we can learn from theology about responses to transgression. In fact, criminologists may find themselves already using the language of religion, with punishment sometimes interpreted as a 'secular penance' (Duff, 2003) or desistance as a form of repentance (Bottoms, 2021).

With redemptive criminology, Pycroft and Bartollas draw on Judaeo-Christian traditions to argue for forgiveness as the starting point of redemption. The book suggests that through forgiveness we allow the other to engage and repent. It is proposed that the other ought to be accepted as an individual, with the whole person embraced. The focus of the book is often the practitioner, for instance the probation officer who 'opens a space of possibility through loving kindness [...] discernment and testing and the thinking of the impossible'. Key influences include the work of René Girard, especially on scapegoats, and the theology of Dietrich Bonhoeffer.

The book overlaps with peace-making criminology and will be of interest to those concerned with how we treat others who have done wrong by society's standards, who have breached society's laws, norms and values.

If taken seriously, a more redemptive criminology will provide a very different understanding of criminal justice, where there is a more therapeutic relationship between practitioner and offender. The book challenges our understandings of rehabilitation and opens the possibility of redemption and forgiveness.

The New Horizons in Criminology book series provides concise authoritative texts which reflect cutting edge thought and theoretical developments in criminology and have an international scope. They are written so that the non-specialist academic, student or practitioner can understand them by explaining principles and developments clearly before going deeper into the subject. There is much within this text that may be unfamiliar for many criminologists; yet the reader is rewarded with a genuinely fresh perspective, a new horizon for criminology.

References

Bottoms, A (2021) 'Criminal Justice and the Ethics of Jesus', in A Millie (ed) *Criminology and Public Theology: On Hope, Mercy and Restoration*. Bristol. Bristol University Press. 21–43

Duff, A (2003) 'Penance, Punishment and the Limits of Community', *Punishment and Society* 5(3): 295–312

Garland, D and Sparks, R (2000) 'Criminology, Social Theory and the Challenge of Our Times', *British Journal of Criminology* 40(2): 189–204

Pycroft, A (2021) 'St Paul Among the Criminologists', in A Millie (ed) *Criminology and Public Theology: On Hope, Mercy and Restoration*. Bristol. Bristol University Press. 71–91

Pycroft, A and Bartollas, C (eds.) (2014) *Applying Complexity Theory: Whole Systems Approaches to Criminal Justice and Social Work*. Bristol. Policy Press

1

Introduction

This book develops and articulates our reading of the Judaeo-Christian concept of redemption, offering sentiment as much as thought on the practices of criminal justice and the role of the practitioner. We are acutely aware that the topics of redemption, and forgiveness, appear marginal to a criminal justice that is ostensibly victim retribution focused and thus are unlikely to become a mainstream discourse; nonetheless, our argument is for the potential for changing the dynamics of practice between individual workers, individual victims and individual criminals, using these resources. Criminal justice practice as a project of modernity has relied increasingly on the use of 'hard', medico-reductionist, 'psy' disciplines (psychology and psychiatry) because they seem to offer scientific objectivity and clarity of meaning, which can then underpin and justify treatment programmes and managerial accountability. The superiority of these approaches is asserted over the 'soft', socially complex, 're' disciplines (rehabilitation, restoration and redemption), which appear too uncertain and contradictory. This book is firmly located in the background noise and messiness of those 're' traditions and through the rereading of foundational texts and the use of hermeneutics seeks to explore the richness of that tradition in the sense of what it means to be human in the face of the 'other'. Our approach enables both an analysis of the failures of the criminal justice system but also provides new (and a retelling of not so new) perspectives and resources for practice in that system. We ground our central message in the dynamic nature of reality. A key argument is that change to the compulsive desire for punishment comes from the 'bottom up' and that the creativity of the criminal justice practitioner enables change to happen at a whole systems level. We are unashamedly placing the subject and subjectivity as central to this narrative and the focus is more on that relationship than the institutional dynamics as we feel that practitioner authenticity is fundamental to the therapeutic relationship.

Ultimately we analyse rehabilitation as a failed utilitarian concept and argue that the dynamics of redemption are much closer to understanding, articulating and achieving an interpersonal justice. The current usage of the word 'redemption' comes from the Latin *redimere*, meaning to buy back something owed, or the clearing of a debt. Also, the old English word *rede* means to give counsel, to advise, and explain. As a root word for 'read' it is also therefore linked to storytelling (significantly in the Qur'an the Angel who appears to the illiterate Muhammad commands him, "Read in the name of your Lord" (Abdel Haleem, 2016 xv)). The Judeao-Christian tradition developed the concept of debt based redemption linked to theories of atonement (see Chapter 4) but the ancient tradition of kinship and the role of the *go'elim* in Judaism provides us with a more nuanced understanding of advocacy and protection that is universalized in the teaching of Jesus of Nazareth (discussed in Chapter 3).

Rehabilitation from the Latin *rehabilitare*, meaning to restore to former privileges, has become the focus of rehabilitation in criminal justice settings. Etymological links with, for example, *habitus* have clear sociological connotations within the modernist and postmodernist imaginations. Theoretically, this addresses the alienation and anomie that are defining features of modernity and which provide some certainty in the face of the fragmentation of the coherent thought structure featuring in some aspects of postmodernism. However, it can be argued that notions of kinship and redemption of property are features of essentially pre-modern societies based on social order and coherence whereas modern responses to crime and transgression are dealing with unwanted relationships between victims and offenders who do not necessarily know each other except via the institutions of justice, for example the drug addict who burgles my house at random, is unknown to me, and only becomes known to me through the processes of adversarial justice. There is nothing relational within this concept other than the connection between the offender, the criminal justice system and its employees as being democratically representative of the victim and wider society. It is a reductionist and utilitarian concept whose ends are not justified by its means (see Chapter 4) as demonstrated by high reoffending rates and the reality that the majority of people in the criminal justice system have no privileges to return to; they are some of the most excluded people on the margins of society. Any alternative has to be able to articulate the relationships between victim, offender and society, including the institutions of criminal justice.

Redemption as first criminology

Within criminal justice there is no framework that enables the speaking of 'truth to power' at the level of the individual practitioner. This speaking truth has traditionally been the role of the prophets, whether secular or religious, but they tend not to fare too well (see Skotnicki, 2021). Nonetheless, called to speak truth, we propose redemptive criminology as the beginning of a first criminology for criminal justice practice. A first criminology articulates our guiding and generative principles, a corner stone upon which our thinking is constructed and where creative and humane practice can be resistant to the normalization of harsh penal measures. If we want a revolution in the practices of justice (and of course not everyone does as some people are satisfied with the totalizing structures therein) then individual workers connecting with other stakeholders (victims, criminals, communities) need to reflect and act on their own potential for resistance and change (see Pycroft, 2019). In large measure this practice requires learning to see what is actually there in encounters within the criminal justice system, and an overcoming of our own socially learned complicity in violence. This battle against ourselves, and our learned thoughts, feelings and behaviours, is the daily work of a lifetime. To achieve this there are rich seams of resources available to the practitioner and this book contributes by looking within and without the criminological canon for inspiration.

We argue for a rereading of redemption as foundational to autonomous, creative and humane practice in the criminal justice system through seeking a genuine encounter between the criminal justice practitioner and the perpetrator of a crime. In particular, a genuinely therapeutic (Gr: *therapeia*, to heal) encounter makes possible a closing of the gap between not just the personal and professional worlds of service users and workers, but also other worlds constituted by victims and communities. Our approach then is universal and collective rather than a reductionist theory of crime, and of necessity decriminalizes criminology (see Shearing, 1989 who argues the necessity of criminology moving away from a focus purely on crime as this now restricts scholarly activity). However, within the current individualistic and retributive context of criminal justice our approach is a *skandalon* (Gr: a scandal, a stumbling block) as it articulates truths to be found within the Judaeo-Christian tradition, and including the truth that this tradition at key historical junctures has justified punishment and harsh penal conditions. It is precisely this paradox of Christianity being both a justification for state power, and increasingly a site of resistance to that state power (see Žižek, 2009b), that we seek to explore.

In orientating ourselves within the criminological canon then our approach is consistent with peacemaking criminology, which, to quote Hal Pepinksy (2013: 320), is concerned with

> [h]ow to transform violence into cooperation, of how to make peace from the intrapersonal to global levels ... (building) ... on literature from all manner of sources ... most of which is by folks who do not call themselves criminologists either ... and a concern for understanding how to transform violence transcends normal academic boundaries.

We also concur with Pepinsky's argument (2013) that peacemaking understands that in crime and criminality there is no political neutrality and that people have locked-in and set agendas, that stories and myths are essential data for understanding the social construction of crime and punishment.

Peacemaking promotes empathy and compassion but the outcomes are very uncertain, with results not always known. This of course is at odds with dominant variations of administrative and utilitarian positivism in the penal sector. Peacemaking criminology has been largely ignored due to a perceived lack of testable hypotheses (see Ishoy and Kruis, 2019) and lying outside of a rationalist episteme with its emphasis on doxastic and wisdom traditions (see Crewe, 2019).

Rather than rejecting the doxastic and wisdom traditions, we see them as essential to understanding both the nature of criminal justice practice and resources for change (see Pycroft, 2020). The pulse of therapeutic inspiration at the centre of this criminology is an exploration of the relationships between myth and reason as expressed in modernity and postmodernity. Myth is a source of collective memory which, when rationally analysed, reveals new understandings of the human condition. This has been understood in, for instance, restorative justice where, for example, ancient and aboriginal sources of communal peacemaking have been researched and in part motivated by failures of the Christian mythos and its support of retributive punishments. We are seeking to rectify this perspective by a re-examination of the Judaeo-Christian tradition guided by Dietrich Bonhoeffer's arguments for 'the non-religious interpretation of biblical terms in a world come of age' (Bethge, 2000: 853). We use Rene Girard's analysis (for example 1978) of religion and the relationships between the violent and the sacred to argue that the 'world come of age' is the 'age of the victim'. This insight provides the necessary epistemological tools to develop Bonhoeffer's arguments and a detailed examination of the meaning of the relationships between victims, offenders, communities and the criminal justice system.

This narrative is a non-sentimental response to the problem of real violence (see Osakabe, 2016) in the wake of modernism, postmodernism and Nietzsche's proclamation of the death of God. We argue that his hermeneutic of suspicion, while necessary, is not able to provide us with a solution to the problem of interpersonal violence that criminal justice perpetuates. Despite modernity's declaration of the death of God, criminal justice systems continue to be the place of the sacred sacrificial that create social order through institutionalized scapegoating mechanisms (see Chapter 3).

If it is possible to speak the name of a god in criminological discourse and criminal justice practice, what is the name that is given and spoken? The triumph of post-Kantian 'Enlightenment' philosophy, with the relegation of religion and faith to the private sphere in liberal democracies, is that every god is legitimate based upon the individual will (see Chapter 3 for a discussion of the Marquis de Sade as the 'flip side' of Kantian thought). An example par excellence is the worldwide 'disbelief' and 'bemusement' that followed from Donald Trump standing in front of a church holding a bible just after threatening military action to quell the rioting following the death of George Floyd in 2020 at the hands of the police. The 'theologization of politics' (see Oughorlian, 2012) means that Trump's god who justifies harsh punishment is no more valid than the god who calls for forgiveness; the god with the most votes wins. In the era that we call modernity the collapse of teleological ethics into utilitarianism conceals these archaic religious mechanisms (see Pycroft and Bartollas, 2018; Pycroft, 2021b) into 'common sense' and 'democratic' justifications for the necessity of punishment and violence. Rarely addressed is the question of 'why punishment is necessary'. Our approach, through seeking a full rationalism of the Judaeo-Christian mythos (Milbank, 2006), is to uncover the obscured names of God, which speak truth and radically disrupt human understanding. In this process of revelation (Gr: *apokaluptein* – see Chapter 4), first, the Girardian analysis reveals that Christianity is not a religion, but an organizing and generative principle that deconstructs the archaic religious. Second, through developing Girard's thought and applying it to criminal justice settings we identify new possibilities for radically changing that violence through a genuine phenomenology of the other disclosed in new readings of sacrifice and gifts to people hitherto seen as 'undeserving'.

We want to insert into criminal justice practice the ontological considerations of what makes humans specifically human, before, outwith or even after the event of crime. Punishment and deterrent sentencing are anti-therapeutic and prevent genuine transformation, in part through perpetuating the myth of rehabilitation (see Carlen, 2013). In bringing about change to counter the locked-in violence of criminal justice processes, then our focus is at the level of the individual practitioner and their understanding of what it means for them to be human in the face of the 'monstrous other'. The scandal of embracing those who should not be embraced (see Chapter 4) is of necessity the role of the criminal justice practitioner (see Nash, 2016 for a discussion of UK police and their self-perceived role as 'scum cuddlers' in working with sex offenders), who requires the personal characteristics and understanding of their own will to power to do this well.

The nature of redemptive and non-redemptive criminology

The key contours of our redemptive paradigm outlined in Table 1.1 are all constitutive of each other in a dynamic and non-linear pattern and emerge in each of the chapters. The way in which we approach, explore and justify each contour is through phenomenology and hermeneutical narrative to reveal and challenge the violence that the deskilling, bureaucratization, routinization and reductionism of much criminal justice practice obscures. Research evidence consistently demonstrates the personal qualities required by practitioners to determine good outcomes from interventions, and yet this area receives the

Table 1.1: Redemptive and non-redemptive criminology

Redemptive criminology	Non-redemptive criminology
Immanence	Metaphysical and normative ethics (teleological or deontological)
Forgiveness	Atonement
Creativity/poiesis	Entropy
Wholeness and being	Reduction and non-being
Grace as gift	Purity codes and sacrifice
Mutuality and empowerment	Coercion and imposition
Unfinished	Platonic return/eternal recurrence of the same

least attention in practice settings. The space that the practitioner opens up for a service user (see Polizzi and Draper, 2013) then depends upon their own ability to know themselves, their strengths and weaknesses, and to be able to catch glimpses of sparks of possibility. The consciousness of the practitioner becomes the focus of activity rather than the service user and hence there is no neutrality in this space or passive phenomenology. It is only through the making of ethical choices that change can emerge or else the status quo is maintained or a race to the bottom instigated. The vocation (Latin, *vocare*, to call) of the criminal justice practitioner is then to locate themselves within the ground of being that emerges between modernity and postmodernity; transcendence and immanence; the sacred and the secular; science and art; thought and language; conformity and creativity. Each designation 'of between' suggests a relationship and co-constitution with the other, which is a relationship of paradox, complexity and emergence.

Phenomenology

In *Being and Time* Heidegger (1978) considers the etymology of phenomenology. *Phainomenon* (from Gr: *phainesthai*) means '[t]hat which appears' or 'that which show itself in, by, as and for itself': and *logos* (from Gr: *legein*), meaning to 'gather together' (this is etymologically linked to *religion* and *spirit*) into the open, to let manifest or appear. Putting these together he understands phenomenology to be the method of letting appear (be seen, become manifest that whose nature it is to appear). In moving beyond reductionism in all its guises phenomenology allows us to examine critically through acts of consciousness those ideas and concepts which are 'taken for granted', including in the practices of justice. Polizzi and Draper (2013: 721) argue that consciousness does not work on many aspects of working in correctional settings, thus 'leaving them phenomenologically unexplored ... the structure of the system, and the dehumanizing effects of the penitentiary'. In the phenomenological tradition those things (objects and events) that are unexplored are left 'manifest' and do not realize their potential. In correctional settings, a therapeutic relationship is required to encounter genuinely the encrustation of what is manifest and to realize their potential through acts of consciousness (Polizzi and Draper, 2013). Texts (stories, myths, scriptures) and narratives transmit events to us, and through this double hermeneutic of using cultural texts to support our interpretations of others' lived experience we seek to engage with that which is manifest.

A note on Heidegger

As referenced in several places throughout this book Heidegger was a Nazi. His influence on criminology and the phenomenological tradition therein has been used extensively and uncritically without referencing the context for his work. We feel it important to justify using his work, which is a core component of the critical and phenomenological tradition in criminology and philosophy, but, as we will argue, that tradition provides us with aspects of critique but definitely not solutions. The evidence for his Nazism has become evident over time as the historical record is published, leading to significant controversy. The idea of a 'good Heidegger' and a 'bad Heidegger' developed, with the former being foundational to the development of post-war French philosophy but with others rejecting his work (see Derbyshire, 2013). Notably Eric Voegelin, a philosopher and contemporary of Heidegger who managed to escape Austria after *Anschluss*, said, '[t]here are not two but one Heidegger. We grow, learn and develop, make mistakes for the best and worst of motives. Whether truly revealed or not, the person of moral guilt remains. Only gift properly conceived can address this'.[1] Central to our conceptualization of redemption is both anamnesis (memory, see later) and gift, and as Eva Kor (see Chapter 5) demonstrates, there is the potential to redeem Nazis, but only through speaking truth. The problem of the truth and its ethical implications after the Holocaust affect many areas of humanities and science. As an example, Eduard Pernkopf's *Anatomy of Man* (see Yee et al, 2019) is a key text for students of anatomy, and investigations in the 1980s and 1990s revealed that Pernkopf had been a committed Nazi. Moreover, among the bodies depicted were victims of Nazi atrocities, but surgeons still rely on this information for procedural planning. Once something is known, it cannot be unknown, no matter how the knowledge has been acquired, and in the case of Heidegger it is not possible to disentangle his philosophical insights from the development of the phenomenological tradition. However we can engage with his work to refute his errors and as Howard Israel (1998) argues with respect to Pernkopf, each individual must then decide how to respond to where the sources of their knowledge have come from.

Hermeneutical narrative

Redemptive criminology provides a heuristic for practice in the real world of criminal justice, and seeks to overcome limitations in contemporary criminological thought, to enable therapeutic empowerment and change. To achieve our aims we develop a hermeneutical narrative that brings new resources to our criminological perspective for the individual practitioner. Heidegger takes hermeneutic (from Gr: *hermeneuein* – and alluding to Hermes, messenger of the gods) to mean 'bringing tidings' a 'making known'. In a process of understanding the complexities of the intersecting worlds and narratives of victims, perpetrators and communities, this approach allows us to occupy liminal spaces '[w]here one tries to get one's bearings as one transits between two (or more) worlds' (Kearney, 2011: xvii). The taken-for-granted processes and justifications for harsh punishments hide these worlds from each other and obscure the relationships between myth and rationality, the sacred and the violent, the universal and the particular. A hermeneutical approach allows us to revisit foundational texts and concepts to un-conceal through modern scholarship meanings and intentions which might have been repressed or obscured. We develop an argument from a hermeneutic of suspicion to one of creativity and affirmation with '[a] multi-world narrative more easily (allowing) for a coherent yet dimensional narrative of construction' (Estes, 2008: 239).

Hermeneutical narrative has developed in continental philosophy, which Critchley argues (1997: 355), 'takes the form of a critical confrontation with the history of philosophy ... with ... a critical dismantling of the tradition in terms of what has been unthought and what remains to be thought'. Critchley (1997: 356) argues that this leads to 'the demand for a transformative practice of philosophy, art, poetry or thinking ... that would be capable of addressing, criticizing and ultimately redeeming the present'. The reader of this hermeneutical narrative is interpreting our interpretations of other people's interpretations. There may be much here in terms of ideas, thinkers and philosophies which are new to the reader, but the invitation is always to engage with the text through thought and research and to explore how these might relate to positive personal actions. All communication is a form of reduction, but in part, we want to counter that reductionism through giving more rather than less. We also want to challenge a tendency to the dumbing down that masquerades as 'accessibility'. Dragan Milovanovic (2019) describes his painful engagement with the work of Jacques Lacan and the need to read and reread until he finally understood. Many of the ideas discussed in our narrative do not and were never intended to complement each other by their authors (who of course were not and could not be aware of each other's existence), it is in this 'edge of chaos' *between* ideas that creativity is found.

We are fully committed to slow thought; after all this book represents the best part of 100 years of cumulative experience, in what we now call 'human services', which cannot be reduced to 'how to do redemption'. The reader is invited to utilize a hermeneutic circle (see Mantzavinos, 2016) whereby they can take research and reflect on the ideas and the meanings that emerge from them within the context of the whole book and the different elements that emerge, to inform and energize their own thought and action. It is only in the lived experience of the reader that these ideas can be actualized so that the criminal justice system can be changed rather than simply interpreted (to paraphrase Marx).

Each of these themes are co-constitutive of the other themes and are indicative of redemption as a dynamic process that is always more than the sum of its parts. The following chapters, each a hermeneutical narrative, are the parts which will constitute our whole argument. These we argue provide us with a framework of redemptive criminology that can be related to practice and the potential for change in overcoming the violence and failures of contemporary justice.

Our narrative focuses on our reading of the Judaeo-Christian tradition and its interface with criminal justice as this is our area of expertise and lived experience. However, we positively encourage the development of this dialogue with other religious and cultural traditions. Any development of religious and philosophical literacy in relation to wider society and the work of the criminal justice system that takes us beyond the merely normative and behavioural is to be welcomed. A key area of focus within these discussions may be related to the concept of personalism (see Chapter 2). As argued by Williams and Bengtsson (2018) the various strains of personalism always relate to the centrality of the person, their reality and experience. They demonstrate that although there are formidable challenges, there are close parallels with western personalism in Jewish, Islamic, Buddhist, Vedantic, Chinese and Japanese thought.

Immanence

A phenomenological apprehension of the other is required to mobilize the energies that enable access to new dynamical states. In developing a genuine phenomenology of the other the problem of ontotheology (see Chapter 2) and metaphysics is addressed to allow for an appreciation of the person in themselves. Immanence is to be with and dwelling within, rather than abstract metaphysical or extrinsic. Methodologically the approach is therapeutic, in engaging with the other, as other, and building a relationship to reduce otherness. Poetic space is immanent, allowing for the development of new dynamical states that are accepting of the person as they are in themselves, in the here and now. In that space the practitioner does not look back to the past as a basis for retribution, or to the future to determine the person that they could become (the binaries of modern criminal justice). The problem of crime is then examined as an event (series of events) that the individual is constitutive of, rather than criminal acts being essentialized so as to define the person by those acts. This non-essentialism opens up a space of possibility to apprehend the individual and their relationships within the implicate order. This is the gift of the practitioner, expressed always as an invitation, non-violent in tone, expression and actions.

Forgiveness

We explore the concept of forgiveness within the context of the relationship between criminal justice, theology and philosophy. Our narrative is in part inspired by the work of Vladimir Jankélévitch, which could be described as an 'asystematic systematicity' Kelley, 2005: xii). His work is enjoying not so much a renaissance in continental philosophy as a genuine discovery as his significant body of thought was overlooked in his lifetime (1903–85). The reason for his being largely ignored was due to his refusal to associate himself with a definite school of thought and he even claimed not to have a philosophy.[2] He was of Jewish descent and barred from holding an academic position in France during the Second World War and there is some evidence that this anti-Semitism continued after the war ended. However, in 1951 he was awarded a Chair in Moral Philosophy at the Sorbonne. He was deeply affected by the Holocaust and the events of the war, and his refusal to engage with the German philosophy that informed the mainstay of French thought (namely Husserl – see Chapter 3; Nietzsche and Heidegger – see Chapter 4 for a discussion in relation to critical criminology) meant that he never became 'mainstream'. Interestingly, while these events caused him to re-examine his Jewish heritage he did not look to either the Torah or the Talmud for philosophical insight in the ways that Martin Buber (2013) and Immanuel Levinas (1969) did for example. In our hermeneutical narrative this is important because while we agree with and develop Jankélévitch's idea that forgiveness is an event, we do not agree that this event is amnesia. Rather the Judaeo-Christian orientation is one of narrative and memory (anamnesis in the theology of Johan Baptist Metz – see Chapter 6), which enables a process of redemption that enfolds past, present and future and which always lays bare and remembers. It is this speaking truth and remembrance of and for the innocent victim *and* the embracing of the perpetrator that constitutes genuine forgiveness and is the scandal of Christianity (see Chapter 4). But likewise, the crimes of the perpetrator are not forgotten and there is an understanding that the 'past' is constitutive of who they are now (see Chapter 5 for a discussion on Paul of Tarsus, a man complicit in murder and repression against the

Jewish sect that became Christianity and following his conversion became the architect of the Church).

Wholeness and being

We develop our hermeneutical narrative and exploration of connectedness at the ontological level by building on developments in complexity theory (the study of non-linear dynamical systems – see Pycroft and Bartollas (2014) in relation to social work and criminal justice), quantum mechanics (see Milovanovic (2014) in relation to criminology) and emergence (phenomena are more than a sum of their parts and cannot be reduced to those parts – see Pycroft, 2014). This is a rich seam of dialogue in overcoming the reductionism and dualism of contemporary thought. Through the work of Kurt Gödel and David Bohm, we will address the problem of the arrow of time and entropy. This chapter provides the justifications for hermeneutical phenomenology and the understanding derived from Gödel that if there is a Platonic realm, we do not have access to it, hence the phenomenological maxim that what we apprehend is first given to us (or emerges to us). Redemption follows from forgiveness expressed as a process of acceptance and wholeness and an immanent apprehension of the other as connected to rather than separate from an implicate order of being, existing prior to the structures, dynamics and powers of the criminal justice system (or any other social context). The implicate order and its relationship to creativity is to be found in the work of the physicist David Bohm (see Chapter 3). This implicate order is enfolded space–time, where time itself is recognized as an illusion and where the person's past, present and future are all enfolded into each other. The practitioner is themself constitutive (enfolded) of (in) this reality and has no objective observer status but nonetheless engages in the difficult work of seeking to grasp 'the almost but not quite' of possibility by working through what is emerging, what is hidden and what can be unconcealed.

Creativity

Creativity focuses on the emergence of new forms and the potential for new forms of living rather than the Newtonian emphasis on entropy or the winding down of life. In our paradigm this is achieved through an act of consciousness whereby the other is understood seen and accepted as *simul justus et peccator* (Martin Luther's phrase meaning literally both saint and sinner) in their space of potentiality, namely what is perceived is both good *and* bad. Chapter 3, through developing a phenomenological perspective, takes Girard's mimetic theory as epistemology. Mimetic theory provides us with an anthropology of violence and an understanding of the relationship between the sacred and the violent in criminal justice. The work of Girard is sensitive to an application of complexity theory and understanding the role of scapegoats as cultural attractors to bring about social order. However, much of this violence is unconscious and is particularly revealed through storytelling and myth in the Judaeo-Christian scriptures.

This acceptance is not an attempt at a complete description of the person in a positivist, metaphysical, essentialist or teleological sense but one that seeks to make sense of the phenomenology of the instant where sparks of possibility are perceived. The practitioner understands that as they have no neutral and objective observer status then they have the potential to be complicit in violence to the other (whether expressed as victim, perpetrator or other members of the community); namely the practitioner, as with every other person, always comes between themselves and that which they apprehend. This understanding builds on the Judaeo-Christian teaching that forgiveness breaks cycles of violence through an excess (we never give up on someone) that overcomes 'the negative measurelessness of evil' (Schwager, 2000: 176). This is apprehended in poetic space (poiesis), which for Bachelard (1969) opens the way to creative imagination requiring active participation with the other and for which there can be no passive phenomenology. He argues that this creativity is independent of causality, and rationality. It is only through poetic space that an irruption of the person in themselves in both being and becoming (expressed as a truth, or series of truth events – see Badiou, 2003) is enabled.

Grace as gift

Redemptive criminology includes gift and repentance through affirmation. Whether the offence is minor or serious, frequently with the assistance of others, the perpetrator comes to a degree of repentance, some more than others. In contrast, non-redemptive criminology turns to purity codes and sacrifice. Purity codes and sacrifice looks to self rather than facing the need for repentant behaviour towards others because of wrongful behaviour. The concept of gift is very much at the heart of the so-called 'religious turn' in continental philosophy and radical hermeneutics (see Kearney, 2011; Kearney and Zimmerman 2016) and, we argue, provides new resources for criminal justice practice. We argue for a conceptualization of redemption as a gift to not just offenders, but also victims and the community; it is not possible for the majority of perpetrators to buy back something owed for a crime committed in a way that would give satisfaction to victims. Therefore, they need to be given resources to enable them to do this, but within a context and framework that acknowledges the problematic of the arrow of time. This approach addresses the past (a crime has been committed and there are victims), the present (the past affects the present and the crime has impacted upon the identities, trajectories and lived experience of all concerned) and the future (there needs to be the potential for new possibilities and identities for all concerned).

Mutuality and empowerment

Our reading of redemption places a heavy emphasis on mutuality and empowerment, which is drastically different from non-redemptive coercion and imposition. Non-redemptive criminology has resulted in brutal and punitive measures of justice. Through providing real-world examples of individuals and organizations who are committed to working in a redemptive way and to bring about change we develop a concept of being-for-others grounded in the theology of Dietrich Bonhoeffer.

Unfinished

Redemptive criminology denies there is a finish line because reality is always emerging, there is no bottom line, only love, life and becoming. Our approach is distinct from the idea of rehabilitation as a return to something, whether expressed in the Platonic and ontotheological sense or as Nietzsche's eternal recurrence of the same. Neither is it a Hegelian-Marxist dialectic whereby the thesis and antithesis dissolve into some new synthetic reality where the past is forgotten. Rather, the hermeneutical narrative that emerges between the self and others is endlessly creative as it draws on shared energies that are gifted to each other and so double, triple and so on as people engage with each other.

It is our hope that this book becomes a focus for debate in challenging the normalization of violence in criminal justice and wider society. We encourage the reader to engage with the text with a critical eye, to hermeneutically develop a narrative of the self. The whole point of hermeneutics is, after all, to have your being challenged and rethought in the light of the other.

2

Immanence and Spaces of Possibility

To quote Martin Luther King Jr, '[t]he fierce urgency of *now*' (Washington, 1986: 167, emphasis added) is our concern. The 'nowness' of redemption enables an analysis of the relationships between the perpetrators of crime, their victims and wider society, and new inclusionary and creative strategies to be informed through a radical awareness of the 'here and now'. The ancient Greek word *arche* denotes a beginning or source of action (for example archaeology) and in the French, the same word denotes a place of safety. Redemption is a space where the infinite (transcendent/virtual) is actualized in the finite (immanent) (von Baltasar, 1990; Shestov, 2016) thus allowing for creativity and innovation and a safe place of being.

Poiesis

This creativity comes from poiesis, as an immanent apprehension of the other. This apprehension (seeing) seeks an actualization (embodiment) of the new by understanding forgiveness as a space of possibility, the place to start rather than the end point (see Chapter 2) of a process. In Greek philosophy *poiesis* is the bringing forth of something new and is the foundation for poetry and poetics. Heidegger saw this making new as emergence in the form of the blossoming of the blossom, or the transformation of the caterpillar into a butterfly. For Plato the new that emerges is a shadow of its true reality, and he rejected poiesis as its creativity was threatening to social order, so much so that he expelled poets from his *Republic* '[b]ecause it has a terrible power to corrupt even the best characters …' (Plato, 2003: 349). For Aristotle emergence is always a form of mimesis (see Chapter 4), with its own inherent potential and drive. Our argument is that poiesis and an occupation of the space of possibility un–conceals (think of the way in which the blossom is revealed through its motion from the inside out) the dynamics of structure (matter), agency (mind) and time, with each enfolded in the other, and is able to differentiate between a non–competitive mimesis and an acquisitive mimesis as the basis of ethical choices (see Chapter 4).

For Bachelard (1969) poetics opens the way for creative imagination requiring active participation with the other and for which there can be no passive phenomenology. Poetic space allows for the development of new dynamical states, which are an immanent acceptance of the person as they are in themselves, in the here and now. This approach is not an imaginary of how a person is in an essentialist sense (the deontology of retribution) (see discussion of ontotheology later), or could be (the teleology of rehabilitation) or an engagement with negative concerns that reinforce either imaginary (the deontology and teleology of risk assessment). This, in the philosophy of Vladimir Jankélévitch (Looney, 2015: 20), means '[n]ecessity and truth are installed as eternally already there and as unengendered self-evidence (*cela-va-de-soi*). But that which posits truth is not itself truth; that which makes the truth the truth is prior to and beyond the dichotomy of true and false' (emphasis in the original). This understanding then opens up the possibilities of a genuine phenomenology of givenness whereby we truly (poetically) understand that the person that we apprehend is first given to us (Marion, 2002), for example the person is a gift to us and our response is an actualization of an anterior gift (see Chapter 6). In this poem 'The Host' William Carlos Williams (1962: 94) reflects on a number of clerics, nuns and evangelists all eating separately in a railway restaurant, saying:

> No one was there
> Save only for the food. Which I alone,
> being a poet,
> could have given them.

Eschatology and teleology

Everything that we experience is in the present. Whatever has gone before, and whatever we perceive as being the basis for moving forward, or whatever we want our future identity to be, is experienced in the present. Lissie Harper (discussed in Chapter 3) could not be clearer about what it means to be a victim of crime, and the continued presence of something precious taken away, while the loss of liberty for the criminal may be only transient within the overall context of their lives; this trauma is experienced in the present. Likewise, we cannot be the person that we were before, or know the person that we will be. Immanence means 'I am' in an eschatological rather than teleological sense. Eschatology is concerned with the end of time (Gr: *eschaton*), expressed usually in Christianity as God's violent judgement to come at the end of the world. The work of Rene Girard is a hermeneutical key (see Chapter 4) to demonstrate that violence always comes from humans and not God, and that the Judaeo–Christian tradition reveals the truth of the potential to violence of 'every person'. This tradition also provides a way out of violence based upon our own anthropic responsibility, rather than abdicating that responsibility to a metaphysical, angry and demanding God (see, Chapter 4; Pycroft, 2021a). Our argument is that the eschaton (see discussion later) makes available everything to us for gifting to the other, in a creative process of actualization and healing relationships. This is akin to Merleau-Ponty's (1968: 151) argument that, '[w]ith the first vision, the first contact, the first pleasure, there is initiation, that is not the positing of a content, but the opening of a dimension that can never again be closed, the establishment of a level in terms of which every other experience will henceforth be situated'.

In contrast *télos* (Gr: end purpose, or goal) defined in both virtue and utilitarian ethics looks to the future not the 'here and now' (see Chapter 6 for a discussion of the problems of teleology for identify formation). For Aristotle the goal of ethics (acquired through rationality) is the *eudaimon* (the good or blessed life) of which virtues (*areté*) are literally notions of excellence, or characteristics that an individual needs to acquire to lead a 'good life'. This excellence is the characteristic to choose the Golden Mean between two extremes, for example courage as a virtue is the mean between cowardice and recklessness. Importantly in Aristotle's ethics (which are inherently elitist and hierarchical), these virtues look towards the end for which we have been created, and so the rediscovery of his texts is used by the medieval scholastics[1] (in Islam, Judaism and Christianity) to underpin a philosophical understanding of what it means to be created by God and how we are ordered towards that creation. This then becomes the basis for natural law conceptions of justice where human law derived from the natural law is itself derived from the divine law, which is promulgated by God, but known through reason.

In contemporary rehabilitative practice the Good Lives Model (GLM) (Ward and Maruna, 2007) focuses on the identification and acquisition of primary human good and is argued to be forward looking and strengths based. The GLM is a therapeutic version of both virtue ethics and strain theory as a teleological conception suggesting that offenders access their primary goods through inappropriate means to realize the goals that society has set.

Utilitarianism represents the tyranny of the majority through its practical applications in justice of the processes of less eligibility (see Sieh, 1989) and risk management, rendering the future unrealizable through a closing down of opportunity and potential through the removal of resources that would allow for the potential to access and realize new dynamical states. This becomes evident in the Risk-Needs-Responsivity (RNR) model of rehabilitation, where considerations of need and how to respond to them are in practice subordinated to risk and public protection considerations. The RNR model is the only model of criminal justice rehabilitation that treats the state as the service user through subordinating human needs to risk considerations (Prof David Polizzi, private correspondence).

This means that victims and communities as well as criminals are prevented from accessing sources of healing through locking in cycles of violence. This is entropic and self-defeating practice as it contains an essential nihilism in that first it assumes the rationality of individual actors and therefore the collective calculus of the greatest happiness for the greatest number to be correct, even, presumably, in the justification of collective violence; but secondly because we cannot say with any certainty in the face of human passions (proclaimed as justified and requiring of satisfaction) precisely where, what or when the end is that truly justifies the means (see Pycroft and Bartollas, 2018). This problem of the entropic nature of utilitarian eschatology contra immanence and creativity is stated by Nelson (1991: 339) when he says that utilitarianism '[i]mplies a surprising prediction about the future, viz, that all experience of pleasure and pain must end once and for all, or infinitely dwindle'.

The space of forgiveness allows for the projection of a virtual image that is immanently actualized now. This is expressed in the philosophy of Henri Bergson, who sought the *elan vital* in the complexity of evolution and in the face of the mechanization and alienation of modernity. He argued that we needed to understand the inner essence of things via empathy and intuition, stating that '[a] true empiricism is that which proposes to get as near to the original itself as possible, to search deeply into its life, and so by a kind of intellectual auscultation, to feel the throbbings of its soul' (Bergson, 1999: 2). In radical and transformative justice, we can utilize Bergson's (1988) development of Aristotle's conception of potentiality (*dunamis*) and its relationship to actuality (*energeia*). This approach, rather than being concerned with someone's power to produce a change (for example to make good through voluntary contrition, or to receive punishment to coerce contrition), is their capacity to be in a different and more completed state (Cohen, 2016) and enabled to be so through the actions of the key stakeholders. While, for example, in desistance theory there is a focus on future selves (new identities) for offenders (for example Hunter and Farrall, 2017; Gålnander, 2019), there also needs to be a future (new identity) for victims (this is the basis of moving from victim to survivor) and communities. Any whole-systems, non-totalizing approach to criminal justice needs to be able to address the dignity and needs of each person concerned and to understand and work with the connections with the other (see later for a discussion of Scheler's personalism).

Redemption is an immediate gift to those whom, according to the combined precepts of purity and rationality, it should not be given. This incongruity and risk of contagion (see Chapter 5) is the *skandalon* of the Judaeo-Christian tradition, the only tradition that offers a radical equality before God and humanity. That gift of redeeming equality revealed in an immanent apprehension of the other is an inaugurated eschatology, a realization of the horizon of identity. The eschaton is the enfolded nature of reality where the trajectories and competing forces of victim, community and offender meet the attractor states of violence (including legal violence), and our own complicity in this. The concept of a pentimento helps to understand this, whereby a painter makes changes to an original painting or sketch and literally repents of the original. However, the original can be discerned or identified by various techniques or is actually visible in the painting itself. In this sense, the painting is a dynamic image where sources can be observed but are not obvious in the presenting image. The 'finished' painting can be analysed using various techniques such as X-ray, infra-red imaging or the application of chemicals to identify the changes, but that history, as interesting as it may be, does not give us the finished picture because owing to its dynamic nature it is always more than the sum of its parts.

The therapeutic encounter with someone who has committed a crime is a form of pentimento, a history that brings them to this point and an image that is unfinished. There is no restoration (return) to an idealized, Platonic and pure original that existed before crime and neither is there an overpainting that hides what has gone before. Everything may be laid bare, but nothing is discarded, everything belongs. As Freud (2001: 61) states, 'in mental life nothing which has once been formed can perish – that everything is somehow preserved and that in suitable circumstances ... it can once more be brought to the light'.

Gnosticism

In the philosophy of Eric Voegelin the concept of the eschaton is central to political science. It is argued by Voegelin (2004) that in the modern world every mass movement and its associated 'ism' (for example Marxism, Fascism and Existentialism) is a form of modern Gnosticism (Gr: *gnosis* meaning knowledge), which, he argues, is anti-philosophical because it seeks to '[i]mmanentize the eschaton'. Voegelin's philosophy is a protest of good against evil based on two principles:

> Philosophy springs from the love of being; it is man's loving endeavour to perceive the order of being and attune himself to it. Gnosis desires dominion over being; in order to seize control of being the gnostic constructs his system. The building of systems is a gnostic form of reasoning, not a philosophical one. First, last and forever, philosophy is the love of wisdom, not its definitive possession. (cited in Voegelin, 2004: XIII)

Gnosticism was a religious movement in the early Christian centuries that emphasized knowledge of God, the nature and destiny of humankind, and how we can be redeemed from the cosmic forces of this world, which imprisons them (including the body) (Wilson, 1983). In this sense, Gnosticism uses mystical and secret knowledge gained from participating in the Godhead (see Underhill, 1960) to escape from the world rather than to deal with the realities of being human. This escape in the form of an appeal to purity from the sinfulness of the world is the antithesis of the incarnation of Jesus Christ, '[w]ho though being in the form of God did not count his equality with God a thing to be grasped' (Philippians 2: 6).

In gnostic thought my secret knowledge is always mine and not universal. In this system, only the adept and the worthy are invited (hence Nietzsche is an elitist, Heidegger a Nazi, and Foucault admires judicial murder – see later and Pycroft, 2021a) contra the kingdom of radical equality of god and humanity based on the Judaeo-Christian God's love. Voegelin affirms our own inability to see our own capacity for evil, but subsequent scholarship does argue that Jesus of Nazareth had immanently inaugurated an eschatology (Dodds, 1980; Barker, for example 2004) (discussed in Chapter 3), with the revelation of the purpose of history being humankind freeing itself from its own violence.[2] This immanence is the space of normative and ethical choices where freedom is not based on secret knowledge but seeing that it is God's radical otherness, which enables me to embrace the other (by not clinging to equality with God), based on reciprocating God's love (see Chapter 4). The infinite expressed in the finite is not the basis of a will to power, but individuation rather than individualism, and for Jankélévitch (Kelley, 2005: xvii),

> life-and thus, time – appears as a succession of choices that we make. Life is then the interplay between the instant where we create and the intervals in which what was created is maintained. The instant – creation – is the demarcation between intervals. It sets the stage for what follows upon it, so to speak.

Likewise, the gospel expressed in the temple theology of the Book of Revelation is one of immanence, where there is no disjunction of structure, agency and time, where Heaven and Earth literally meet (see Barker, 2004). An appreciation of this dynamic and its application to anthropic responsibility rather than an abdication to metaphysical judgement (see Pycroft, 2021a; 2021b) requires a sense making based on an understanding of a God beyond all ontotheological determination (for example unlike the Gods of Olympus, who are created in our own image and thus justify violence) (Marion, 2012, discussed in Chapter 4).

In the philosophy of Romano Guardini (2013: 19), each moment of existence is an historic centre with each person '[g]iven the burden of choice in that crucial and irreducible drama of existence itself', with these encounters piercing time and revealing eternity. The revelation of the nature of that eternity is in a reintegration of the modern with the postmodern and the rediscovery of change agency (see Milovanovic, 1997) (for example Milovanovic's (2014) Quantum Holographic Criminology uses Lacanian psychoanalysis in combination with quantum mechanics to explore the relationships between mind, matter and creativity).

Individualism and criminal justice

Western criminal justice systems grounded in the individualistic traditions of western philosophy and retributive theology result in offender-centred concepts of justice and use adversarial approaches to find the truth (Liu, 2017). This adversarial reality is mimetic, leading to a locking in (see later) of retribution and the perpetuation of cycles of violence that disadvantages everybody. Redemption, by contrast, is concerned with wholeness and inclusion in all relationships. It implies connectedness between people and the necessity of right relationship between those people in a way that addresses the arrow of time, the problems of the past and possible futures. In criminal justice as it is currently practised the arrow of time is expressed in the form of looking to the past (to determine just and proportionate retribution), addressing the present (to give satisfaction to victims and securing the rights of victims and perpetrators), and looking to the future (including rehabilitation, risk management and public protection).

The processes of justice seek to determine beyond reasonable doubt the events that took place and the moral culpability of those involved. However, there is no Platonic reconstitution after those events, and no possibility of securing a truly objective picture of what occurred, or measure of moral culpability even for those directly involved. Reductionism is furthered by a tendency to utilize the arrow of time to prioritize either victims or criminals, and to the exclusion of each other. As the past is not retrievable there is first a deontological (universally idealist) judgement that the rights of the victim have been transgressed coupled with a valuation of what has been experienced or lost by victims and what is due to them (and society) from the perpetrators in terms of sentence served, its type (custodial, non-custodial and so on) and any other forms of compensation. This valuation is grounded in utility, with the teleological argument of the end justifying the means, relative to the greatest happiness principle. The ideals of the Enlightenment sought to develop a rational society that guaranteed individual rights (liberalism) and which over time saw the development of democracy to secure those rights (liberal democracy). This rationality was to be free from the myths of religion and an increased separation between Church and state, with religion being reduced to the status of the individual's right to belief, and having no influence in the public sphere.

Haecceity and ontotheology

Our approach argues that we can apprehend and articulate the haecceity, the 'thing in itself' (*thisness*, see, for example, Porter, 2005 for an analysis of scholastic approaches to natural law) of redemption which Enlightenment philosophy, and liberalism since Kant, has rejected. Both Kant and Heidegger use the term 'ontotheology' in ways that are independent from each other but nonetheless have some loose connections (see Haltemann, 1998). In Kantian rationalism (namely, the sovereignty of reason, and metaphysics as the domain of that reason) ontotheology represents knowledge of the existence of God[3] through reason alone without recourse to natural revelation or scripture (for example we hold the truths of the pursuit of life, liberty and happiness to be self-evident). Kant's ethical (practical reason) rather than theological (falling outside the remit of practical reason) arguments are focused on personal autonomy and the intent of the individual to will the universal good (categorical imperative). This is achieved through imposing their own limits rather than allowing others (including God) to impose those limits (forming the basis of liberalism, and versions of postmodern thought). In this respect Kant is responding to the new physics of the Enlightenment (see Rohlf, 2016) which saw nature and matter as mechanistic (deterministic) and the Cartesian dualism of separating structure and agency. In contrast, Heidegger uses the term 'ontotheology' to critique the general approach to western philosophy that had followed Plato, who had sought a metaphysical mastery of reality. This mastery is an essentialism that explains the existence of individuality through the imposition of universal ontological forms, which in turn emanate from a theological conceptualization of the Good that is the source of everything.

The contemporary philosopher and theologian Jean-Luc Marion (2012) argues that the problem with ontotheology is that the nature of being and the way it is represented takes precedence over the very being itself. Marion finds the origins of ontotheology in Descartes, who had shifted philosophy from the ontological orientation of medieval scholasticism to that of epistemology (see Scruton, 2003). Foundational to Enlightenment and subsequent thought is the rejection of haecceity, whereby we could now only describe rather than engage with the thing in itself. In applying this logic to criminal justice, we can see how it uses an epistemology of agency to determine a metaphysical structure to the person, without engaging with the truth in itself of that person or their circumstances. The humanity or the personness of the person are lost but a new reality (judgement) of that person is created, based upon what is epistemologically valid according to my own frame of reference. This epistemic (mechanical and disjunctive) turn was further reinforced by Kant's practical reason and leads to consciousness *of* (separate from) rather than *in* (connected to) something. This situation remained until the work of Henri Bergson, whose philosophy was an attempt to overcome Kantian antinomies by asserting the possibility of absolute knowledge and is reinforced by developments in hermeneutical phenomenology, quantum mechanics and complexity theory, which have revealed the dynamic nature of reality that we are constitutive of (see Pycroft, 2018).

Kant argues that humans are rational and autonomous by nature and that in practice we can determine normative limits on human actions. However, Kant's idealism gives rise to antinomies (as we cannot apprehend the thing in itself), thus, the validity of every differing perspective leads to a reification of *la différence* itself (see Žižek, 2009) and ultimately the breakdown in coherent thought structure that is represented in some aspects of postmodernism.

Individualism within the context of punishment and rehabilitation, then, stems from a reductive mindset, expressed as scientific positivism, idealist ethics and the utilitarian calculus. Complexity theory (see Pycroft and Bartollas, 2014) addresses the non-reducible and dynamic nature of reality, thus allowing for an exploration of human nature where context really does matter and having profound implications for criminological method. In moving towards a whole system (complexity based) understanding then the relationships between structure and agency are treated as a duality (see Walklate and Hopkins, 2019) rather than the Cartesian 'ghost in the machine' approach to splitting the universe between thinking substances (*res cogitans*) and the mechanical world (*res extensa*). This requires the development of a new language based on a relational approach for example the New Asian Paradigm of Criminology (Liu, 2017) contra western (occidental) reductionism. Within this approach, the dynamics of time are also important.

Reductionism, fragmented thought and the implicate order

The physicist David Bohm (1980) cogently argues for the reasons why western thought is fragmentary in nature rather than holistic (in the course of his argument he also points out that the Anglo-Saxon words 'hale' and 'holy' come from the same root as 'whole'). Bohm's arguments concerning the nature of reality as undivided wholeness in flowing movement and the subsequent illusion of fragmentation are important in our analysis of the relationship between myth and reason, in scientific method. For Bohm the fundamental problem for humanity arises from our almost universal habit of thinking that our thought corresponds with objective reality. What he is outlining is a version of epistemic fallacy whereby we confuse the theories and models that we use to look at the world with actual knowledge (form) of how the world is. Therefore, we take a theory such as Newton's exposition of the material universe and it gives us a radically new and different understanding of nature, in comparison to what had gone before. This theory worked until the 20th century and the discovery of relativity and quantum theory. Again, radically new perspectives are provided through these theories, which modify the scope of the previous Newtonian model. Bohm argues that we are constantly developing new and updated forms of insight, which give us a clarity to a point. However, importantly these approaches are worldviews rather than a true knowledge of how things are. Importantly, as Bohm argues, there can be no conclusive experimental truth about the truth of falseness of a general hypothesis seeking to cover the whole of reality.

A genuine therapeutic encounter with the other is the phase space within the criminal justice system, with the possibility of revealing the real and implicate order (see later) where there is a potential for revelation (un-concealment) for victims, perpetrators and communities. The concept of phase space is outlined by Mackenzie (2005: 52–3): 'Phase space trades off time for space. It very literally renders (what) Kauffman calls "a space of possibilities" ... But the trade-off is the loss of "natural" or common-sense Euclidean space.' An implicate order (Bohm, 1980) demonstrates an ontology, epistemology and ethic of connectedness between reality and thought and crucially between people and their environments. The key to Bohm's argument is

> the notion of the enfolded or implicate order. The essential feature of this idea ... (is) ... that the whole universe is in some way enfolded in everything and that each thing is enfolded in the whole. From this it follows in some way, and to some degree everything enfolds or implicates everything, but in such a manner that under typical conditions of ordinary experience, there is a great deal of relative independence of things. The basic proposal then is that this enfoldment *relationship* is not merely passive or superficial. Rather it is active and essential to what each thing is. It follows that each thing is internally related to the whole, and therefore to everything else. The external *relationships* are then displayed in the unfolded or implicate order in which each thing is seen, as has already been indicated, as relatively separate and extended, and related only externally to other things. The explicate order, which dominates ordinary experiences as well as classical (Newtonian) physics, thus appears to stand by itself. But actually, it cannot be understood properly apart from its ground in the primary reality of the implicate order. Because the implicate order is not static but basically dynamic in nature, in a constant process of change and development, I called its most general form the holomovement. All things found in the unfolded, explicate order emerge from the holomovement in which they are enfolded as potentialities and ultimately fall back into it. They endure only for some time, and while they last, their existence is sustained in a constant process of unfoldment and re-enfoldment, which gives rise to their relative stable and independent forms in the explicate order'. (Bohm, 1990: 3, emphases in the original)

Within Cartesian dualism there is the assumption that matter occupies discrete space whereas mind does not. Quantum mechanics challenges that assumption with Bohm's theory developing the argument that the particles of physics have primitive mind-like qualities, thus it is not possible to make an absolute distinction between mind and matter. In developing accounts of reality that correspond to contextual, qualitative and connectionist models (contra independent, quantitative and representational models), then, Bohmian theory offers real potential in developing and understanding of relationships. He argues (see Bohm, 1980; Bohm and Hiley, 1987; Bohm, 1990) for a new kind of quantum field. In physics, these quantum fields can be represented as potentials, which describe a field as a potentiality, present at each point of space acting on a particle, or, for our argument, human beings. Crucially it is the active communication from within the whole system (quantum field) that gives shape and form to the particle. The ways in which these particles interact is dependent upon the pool of information within the whole system but in ways that cannot be pre-assigned. The quantum potential for a whole system is then non-local and brings about order or form (or 'emergence' to use the language of complexity theory).

With respect to what we experience in the classical world of physics as opposed to quantum-level behaviour Bohm (1990) argues for wholeness at the quantum level and objective significance. We argue that this applies to the individual as well. He argues that active information is the rudimentary mind-like behaviour of matter, given that the essential quality of mind is the activity of form rather than substance. In this theory, active information is both physical and mental in nature in a relationship that continues to exist at infinite levels of subtlety, and our consciousness and thought forms are present at the quantum level. The implications of this approach are profound in which there is no division between mind, matter and consciousness, with our whole beings engaging in a 'a flux of fundamental participation' (Bohm, 1990: 9). Bohm (1990) argues that both 'mind' and 'matter' serve only as terms for analysis, which help us to understand things, but cannot be seen as separate substances in interaction with each other or reduced to serve as a function of the other.

Paul Cilliers (2005), likewise, in his development of complexity theory in the light of postmodern thought, seeks to avoid an approach to the dynamic nature of reality that is not purely relativistic. For Cilliers it is far more important to think in terms of relationships between the parts of a system and its whole rather than deterministic rules. This is because of the significance of the observer within the system, which is open and has unclear boundaries, which in themselves should not be confused with the limit or influence of the system. The diversity of the system is the best resource for understanding the system rather than a reduction to component parts; significantly self-organization and social construction undermine the concept of self-contained atomized subjects beloved of Cartesian science; and because we do not have neutral observer status we have to make choices and engage in normative considerations.

A phenomenology of the implicate order

Having articulated that a connection between things exists at an ontological level we need to more fully outline the phenomenological necessity for addressing consciousness within the implicate order at the human level. To start, this comes from mathematics with Gödel's Incompleteness Theorems (see Raatikainen, 2015, demonstrating that it is not possible to find a complete and axiomatic set across all mathematics). Gödel's first theorem states that within a mathematical system it is not possible to find a system that is capable of proving all truths about the relationships of the numbers within that system: there must be statements about natural numbers that are true but are not provable within the system. The second theorem states that such a system cannot demonstrate its own consistency. These findings have been nothing short of revolutionary in mathematics and beyond and have led to the view that a complete theory of the universe is not possible. In part this is due to our lack of overall observer status (for example a rejection of the 19th-century Pierre-Simon Laplace's positivist conceit of the Daemon; the intellect that could know all past events, predict all future events and understand any composite entity through a process of atomizing the constituent parts), thus our systems are always self-referential. However, as Gödel also demonstrates, it is not possible to formulate a theory of the universe in a finite number of statements (http://www.hawking.org.uk/godel-and-the-end-of-physics.html).

Gödel's mathematics is inherently complex and reveals the limitations of classical mechanics, positivism and knowledge. In addressing these 'problems' his philosophy is also complex, in which he defended both the rationalist idea that mathematics is a description of Platonic objective reality *and* the realist concept of the impossibility of interpreting empirical laws due to the fact that our sense data are bound up with the conditions under which they are experienced. This gives rise to the fascinating tension that the objective Platonic realm exists, but that the only access we have to it is through what itself emerges, from it, to us. This means that no correspondence or verification about those conditions and the statements that we want to prove can be made. To try to overcome this dualism Gödel looked to phenomenology and stated as follows:

> [T]here exists today the beginning of a science which claims to possess a systematic method for such a clarification in meaning, and this is the phenomenology founded by Husserl. Here

clarification of meaning consists in focussing more sharply on the concepts concerned by directing our attention in a certain way, namely onto our own acts in the use of these concepts, onto our own powers in carrying out our acts, etc. But one must keep in mind that this phenomenology is not a science in the same sense as other sciences. Rather it is (or in any case should be) a procedure or technique that should produce in us a new state of consciousness in which we describe in detail the basic concepts we use in our thought or grasp other basic concepts unknown to us. I believe there is no reason at all to reject such a procedure at the outset as hopeless ... not only is there no reason for the rejection (of phenomenology), but on the contrary one can present reasons in its favour. (Gödel, 1995: 383, cited in http://plato.stanford.edu/entries/goedel/goedel-phenomenology.html)

Phenomenology and the unconscious

In the phenomenological tradition following Husserl there is an understanding that that which we apprehend is first given to us (Marion, 2002a). However, the phenomenology of Husserl is a philosophy of consciousness, which is descriptive and unable to gain access to the unconscious (see Richardson, 1980). In the language of complexity theory, what we apprehend is an emergent event, and our consciousness is not separate from that emergence. Not only do we have consciousness in rather than of the person (see Pycroft, 2018) (Chapter 3) but there is already a connection that has the potential to change the trajectory of that relationship and its outcomes. In addition, reality does not emerge from a single source but rather the Platonic, the classical level of physics, the quantum and time are enfolded in each other. The process philosophy of Bergson and the development of his concept of time and consciousness as *la durée*, or 'duration' (Bergson, 1988) are useful in understanding the connectionist nature of the complex systems in criminal justice constituted by victims, offenders, communities and workers. Within *la durée* Bergson differentiates between quantitative (discrete) and qualitative (continuous) multiplicities. Hodges (2008: 409) describes these differences as follows:

Quantitative multiplicities are numerical in nature and take the form of the one and the many: their chief differences are homogeneous differences of *degree*, and such multiplicities can therefore be divided without occasioning a difference in kind. Qualitative multiplicities, by contrast, on division create heterogeneous differences ... they comprise an interrelated (i.e.

relational) infinite whole, where any multiple is fused with all other multiples and anyone cannot either be isolated or change without all others changing. (emphasis in the original)

To enable a whole system change we have to engage in a process of intuition that allows us to enter into the thing that will allow for absolute knowledge. However, in line with Gödel we have to say that this absolute knowledge is not possible, as intuition (to be understood as self-sympathy and empathy for the other) only gives us knowledge of *la durée* as a contracted part of the whole, but nonetheless is related to the whole, and its becoming. Within Bergson's approach 'there is no direction in which flux or process is moving, and there is no one river of time that flows' (Hodges, 2008: 415), which would appear to be consistent with Einstein's theory of relativity but again the dynamics of the system are relative to the arrow of time as a quantitative multiplicity; evolution is not reversible. The flow of time and our experience of it is dependent upon our position within the criminal justice system; sometimes it appears to go fast and at other times to be slowing down.

Novum and natality

Qualitative multiplicities allow for a therapeutic space of possibility rather than reductively focusing on the punishment of individual transgression. This is akin to what Ernst Bloch (Goldman and Thompson, 2019) describes as the *novum*, and Hannah Arendt *natality*. The novum, or the genuinely new, distinguishes itself from a repetition of the old (in both the Platonic sense of reconstitution and the Nietzschean sense of eternal recurrence) (see Chapter 4). Bloch argues for the creation of a concrete utopia based upon the underlying dynamics of the energy of matter in action, not in an abstract sense, rather based upon our knowledge of the world, its possibilities and the embracing of hope. Within Bloch's thinking the process connections between past, present and future enable the world to be in a radically different state to where it is now based upon an *ex materia* and non-metaphysical reality. Despite his materialist Marxism, the concern for Bloch is not the negation of religious belief but the creative possibilities that become available through re-appropriating religious experience. In this sense the past, its philosophies and theologies become an inheritance filled with undiscovered and dormant human hopefulness (see Green, 1969). For both Marx and Bloch religion was to be anthropologized but the fact remains that religion, while a manifestation of human alienation (see Chapter 4), has been the strongest protest against this alienation (see Žižek', 2009b). Therefore, 'for Bloch the question of God is by definition the question of man ... and for him the progressive insertion of man into the center of concern and the dethronement of the gods is one of the most important leitmotivs of the western liberal tradition'

(Green, 1969: 129–30). In this perspective, the focus becomes the Kingdom of God (as the place of human potential) and a movement away from God, with God disappearing and being replaced by Christ, who is, however, no ordinary mortal. Christ becomes *homo absconditus* where he 'projects himself into the Above … not as man in his present state, but as the Utopia of a possible humanity whose core and eschatological brotherliness he has proleptically demonstrated' (Bloch, 1951 cited in Green, 1969: 33).

Bloch was seeking to integrate the physics of Aristotle into Marxism via the Aristotelian Left. He saw (in the dialectical sense) Christianity as the antithesis of Marxism. He is critical of both for becoming stagnant whether through Marxism's neglect of utopian impulses contained within art, culture and religion but dismissed as bourgeois, or as aspects of false consciousness or Christianity allowing itself to become the state religion and complicit in servitude. Bloch develops his philosophical genealogy from Aristotle via the Islamic scholars Ibn Sīnā and Ibn Rushd. The medieval scholastic Christian philosophers (particularly Thomas Aquinas) were indebted to them for their translations of Aristotle. The latter, Bloch argues provide a right-wing version of Aristotle and the development of a mechanistic view of reality where ideas (idealism) and its arbiters, clerical authority, are absolute.

In contrast the Left Aristotelian view (through the Islamic lens of Ibn Sīnā and Ibn Rushd) (see Goldman and Thompson, 2019) focuses on removing the 'metaphysical whip' of the threat of hell in both Christianity (see Chapter 6) and Islam (the soul does not outlive the body and is therefore not sentient), thus removing clerical power to subordinate the masses. Significantly in both Ibn Sīnā and Ibn Rushd there is a focus on the active intellect of all people rather than cognitive elites, thus democratizing access to truth. Finally, the relationship between matter and form is reshaped, which allows matter (the world) to change beyond fixed categories and to develop latent possibilities (see the discussion on transubstantiation in Chapter 7). Bloch argues for a meta-religious atheism that realizes Marx's vision of naturalized man and humanized nature and a final eschatological reconciliation of subject and object that has immediate expression in the moment of experience (Green, 1969).

Space, including therapeutic space, is not neutral, and empty possibilities and potential can be for good or for bad. As Hamlet says, '[t]here is nothing either good or bad, but thinking makes it so' (Shakespeare, 1975), and an immanent acceptance of those whom society says should not be accepted is always challenging and difficult. Arendt (1961), in discussing the arrow of time (she was a student of Heidegger who supervised her doctoral thesis on St Augustine), argues that both the past and the future are forces which act on the present. The person is inserted not into this time but into a gap in time which is kept in existence by a constant fight against past and future. It is in this gap that we can insert new beginnings (natality) by differentiating between time and space; our freedom dissociated from time is associated with space. Importantly we are not talking here of a timeless, idealized, Platonic space but one that has a spatial dimension (Arendt, 1961). Arendt is correct to identify that this natality is based on principles of conjunctive rather than disjunctive forces, but this insight (which is dialectical) needs developing further as the gap can too readily take the form of a 'carnival of atrocity' (see Miller, 1990) where difference, competition and a Girardian false transcendence is based upon violence against a scapegoat (see Chapter 4), which is seen as justified in maintaining that space.

Personalism

In addressing the relationship between the part and the whole, and considering issues such as personalism, community, solidarity, phenomenology and religious experience, the philosophical anthropology of Max Scheler is a further and important resource in developing our hermeneutical and phenomenological narrative. As a pioneering phenomenologist, Scheler sought to save philosophy from both reductionist positivism and American pragmatism (a variant of utilitarianism defining human beings as nothing more than *homo faber* (toolmakers) (Davis and Steinbock, 2018)) by arguing for phenomenology as an attitude rather than a method. Through this attitude and by loving trust the world itself is given, with Scheler arguing that philosophy is concerned with loving participation whereby humans are motivated not by lack (in the Girardian sense of desiring what the other has – Chapter 4) but by wonder at the sheer abundance and inexhaustibility of the world. This wonder includes a discovery of the 'other' and a willingness to be open to who they are. This love (*agapē* rather than Eros) is always directed to the infinite, absolute value and being.

The contribution of Scheler's phenomenology of religious experience is argued by Davis and Steinbock, 2018 (https://plato.stanford.edu/entries/scheler/):

> Scheler's insistence on the possibility of a phenomenology of religious experience, an insistence that it is possible to provide a description of the essential qualities and conditions of the experience of the holy, is itself a critique of modernity and of the positivistic tendencies growing in philosophical and scientific thought.

For Scheler, the failure of modernity is to rely on the mode of rational proof as only being objective or true, whereas phenomenology is open to distinctive modes of evidence, including the evidential mode of revelation. As with Girard, Scheler grants revelation its own integrity and treats it as meaningful within the context of rational investigation. In Enlightenment thought those normative considerations, expressed, as ethics (deontology, virtue, utilitarian), sees no veil between the conscious and the unconscious, only the purity and supremacy of the rational. The value of religion, including to the state, is in behaviourism and social order; Nietzsche reveals this historical crisis of Christianity, and psychoanalysis uncovers the state of the soul of modernity and its collective psychosis. Freud calls for a more scientific understanding of the individual psyche whereas Jung argues the need to return to that which myth reveals in the collective unconscious. The work of Girard straddles both (see Chapter 4). For Scheler the givenness of the divine is its demonstration, but if Gödel is correct in postulating the existence of a Platonic realm that we do not have access to then we are reliant on what emerges (is given to us) from that realm and which we can apprehend. This is God descending (the incarnation) rather than man ascending (Jesus as *homo absconditus*, or Nietzsche's *Übermensch*) and in a sense, both are emerging. This is articulated in the temple theology of the Book of Revelation, which clearly states '[t]he home of God is among mortals' (Revelation 21). The logic and spirit (*logos*) of the incarnation is that God has become man in the form of Jesus Christ as a gift from the God who is beyond both the physical and the metaphysical. A God without being (Marion, 2012) (see Chapter 4) who asserts rather than negates our human responsibility to each other by revealing unity through violence at the heart of culture and providing a solution to that violence through *imitatio Dei*. The critical tradition in criminology cannot provide a solution to this violence, in fact it perpetuates it (see Chapter 4).

Scheler's philosophy develops into a personalism which Whitehead and Crawshaw (2013: 589) argue provides a 'coherent academic expression ... where human beings have innate and irreducible value and, from this position, it is deduced that persons should be approached as ends, not means – always subject, never an inanimate object, thing or impersonal "it"'. This personalism understands that every human is an exceptional person because they simply are and thus enables us to move beyond violence in our relationships.

The concept of personalism enables us to develop concepts of wholeness as distinct from perfection and purity. The former is Judaeo–Christian, the latter is ancient Greek (particularly Plato). Personalism in its various guises always asserts the primacy of the person as the basis for investigation, their haecceity, with, for example, Deleuze and Guattari (Smith and Protevi, 2008) using this concept of the medieval philosopher Duns Scotus to develop modes of individuation that are non-identity based and which are dynamic and relational. Williams and Bengtsson (2018) argue that personalism focuses on the significance, uniqueness and inviolability of the person in their relations and social dimensions. It represents schools of thought where the person themself and their dignity are the ontological and epistemological starting point of philosophical reflection. This requires an appreciation of the inherent 'value' of the person as 'someone' and not 'something', for example in criminal justice we apprehend the individual whatever their designation as victim or offender as the person that they are in themself. Further, each individual deserves to be treated by virtue of their inherent dignity. Williams and Bengtsson (2018) state it thus:

> When the person is the object of one's action, a whole ethical structure enters into play that is absent when the object of one's action is a thing. How persons should be treated forms an independent ethical category, separate in essence and not only in degree from how non-persons (things) are to be treated.

So far, so Kantian, so transcendental. However, Deleuze requires this Kantian perspective in relation to personalism and the formation of identity to have an immanent actualization in terms of what is radically new. This radical newness aims at production rather than representation and in conjunction with Bergson's Creative Evolution suggests the following (Smith and Protevi, 2008):

> [T]here is not less but more in the idea of the possible than in the real, just as there is more in the idea of nonbeing than in that of being, or more in the idea of disorder than that of order. When we think of the possible as someone 'pre-existing' the real, we think of the real, then we add to it the negation of its existence, and then we project the 'image' of the possible into the past. We then reverse the procedure and think of the real as something more than possible, that is, as the possible with existence added to it. We then say that the possible has been 'realised' in the real. By contrast, Deleuze will reject the notion of the possible in favor of that of the virtual. Rather than awaiting realisation, the virtual if fully real, what happens in genesis is that the virtual is actualized.

This actualization rather than realization happens through immanent power, which is not a dominating power, but the ability to act and to form assemblages and an emerging multiplicity in unity, that is the becoming of identity. In Judaeo-Christianity, this giving of life is always a consummation, a meeting with the other that is possibility (*dunamis*) itself and which does not subtract through diminution but is excessive in its giving. This is the basis for understanding the superabundance of the economy of grace (discussed in Chapter 5).

3

The Dynamics of Forgiveness

The starting point for redemption is forgiveness, which is the space of possibility where we actualize new possibilities for people through meeting them as they are in themselves. We take forgiveness as our starting point of action (*arche*) rather than end (*telos*). Why? Because to repent (see Chapter 5) people need forgiveness first, with subsequent repentance reciprocated and reinforced (see Braithwaite, 2016; Fiddes, 2016 in relation to forgiveness and restorative justice). In Judaism the Hebrew word *avon* means both crime and punishment (von Kellenbach, 2013), with crime being harmful to both the victim and the offender. Within Judaism, the possibility of repentance is a basic human need, so much so that God created it before he created the world, as without it humanity could not exist (Ronel and Ben Yair, 2018).

Forgiveness is not a conditional formula, an operationalization: As Verdeja (2004: 26) states, 'as forgiveness becomes instrumentalized, it is drained of its transformative power and simply becomes a tool in larger political and social projects. It ceases in other words to be a moral action in its own right when it is appended to broader moral or political ends'. Forgiveness opens the space of possibility and provides for a genuine encounter where there is no distinction between structures, agency and time (see Chapter 2). Forgiveness counters the negatively reinforcing failures of rehabilitation and enables a process of redemption that is a higher-order (non-reductionist and non-metaphysical) solution to problems perpetuated by the culturally determined problems of revenge. This desire for metaphysically justified revenge expressed as the need for satisfaction (see Chapter 4) is entropy and dissipation of the self. In the Cohen Brothers' film of Cormac McCarthy's (2005) novel *No Country for Old Men*, the Sheriff tells his father that the man who had shot him and left him in a wheelchair had died in prison, and wants to know what his father would have done if he had been released. The father replies '[n]othing' and when the Sheriff expresses surprise, the father responds, '[a]ll the time you spend tryin' to get back what's been took from you there's more goin' out the door. After a while you just try and get a tourniquet on it.' This is not an expression of forgiveness, but an understanding that revenge will not change harms caused, or discover new and creative energy, but, rather, will dissipate what remains.

The dynamic energy of forgiveness is always in the spaces between the victim, the perpetrator and communities. These liminal spaces allow for a process of redemption. Redemption as a process *begins* with forgiveness, literally something given first, before or upfront in the face of the moral guilt of the other. Without guilt, there is no requirement for forgiveness or redemption, and the Judaeo-Christian perspective is that we are all complicit in violence in one form or another and all need to engage in repentance, which we define as at least an acknowledgement of the gift of forgiveness (see Chapter 5). The energy required for forgiveness is not a subtraction for any of the people involved, but is a genuine other-focused space between each that is free of my own desire for even legally justified violence. This space is where we meet each other as truly human in an ontological reality free of all determinations, where the other is in themself and I am.

The unforgiven, and those who are not able to forgive, by necessity live a double life (see Alison, 2003). They are reduced, rather than whole, and experience the non-being (discussed later) of separation within the self, with non-being constantly undermining being (we accept the scholastic view that *esse qua esse bonum est* – being as being is good). For the victim this is experienced through a range of negative emotions and traumas, and re-traumatization. For the offender the 'lock in' of criminal behaviour become a basis for judgements about people's failures to change, with questions focused on their motivation and moral agency. As only that which is seen as worthy or pure is embraced, the truth of the person as they are in themself is not embraced. It is this failure to embrace that becomes the necessary basis for the sacred ideology and idolatry of punishment with increasingly harsh measures and the withdrawal of human resources in modern justice systems. Redemptive change occurs within social settings so this embracing is not the responsibility of the victims but is a community responsibility to help both victim and offender to find ways of giving to each other (see Chapter 5). In Jungian terms an integration of the shadow is required, and as much for society as for the victim and offender. Maruna et al (2004: 286) suggest that there are several possibilities related to what constitutes shadow: '[a] sense of inferiority or shame at our own insignificance; guilt over our own role in the creation of the crime problem; sublimated jealousy and admiration for the criminal's exploits; sadistic impulses to humiliate others; and guilt regarding our own sexual desires'. This approach is a deeply individual understanding of shadow whereas the scapegoat mechanism reveals its social aspects to resolve communal crises (see Chapter 5). The sacrifice or expulsion of the other is a projection of the unconscious shadow onto vulnerable people. In criminal justice the apparent rationality and structure of normative ethics (whether deontological, virtue or utilitarian) not only prevents us from accessing and understanding the unconscious drive for revenge (see Chapter 3), but in its individualism prevents us from thinking of the excessive giving that is the cornerstone of Judaeo-Christianity as a solution to those problems.

Hayden and Gough (2010) revealed a type of mechanized dynamic that is typical of creative intentions losing their power to transform in the everyday realities of the bureaucratic. Their research into the use of restorative justice in children's homes demonstrates how this intervention becomes a form-filling and tick-box exercise. The creative practitioner is facilitating something despite the dynamics of non-being (see Chapter 4) at play in the criminal justice system that is bearing down on them. They are themself (and in themself) constantly fighting against the forces that seek to close down possibilities (see Chapter 7), therefore a more detailed understanding of the nature and dynamics of that space becomes necessary.

The contested nature of forgiveness

The meanings, desirability and value of forgiveness are contested, both in theology and philosophy (see Griswold, 2007). Theologically, concepts of forgiveness have become bound up with doctrines of atonement, whereby forgiveness has to be earned, which has had a significant impact on processes of retributive justice (see Chapter 3). Philosophically, for Nietzsche (2003) forgiveness particularly as expressed in Christianity is no more than a slave mentality, the revenge of the weak against the strong.

For Derrida (2002) the impossibility of forgiveness means that it can only be reserved for extreme evil and is therefore meaningless in everyday life, whereas for Ricoeur (2004) it is difficult but not impossible. For some years prior to his death in 2004, Derrida pursued seminars between California and Paris that took particular foci, interweaving certain themes, including forgiveness, the death penalty, sovereignty and theology. At the heart of these apparently different strands of Derrida's late work is the constant thematic of the impossible, that which absolutely cannot be achieved. Thus, forgiveness is only possible on the basis that what has been done to someone is impossible to forgive. In other words, forgiveness must be unconditional (Derrida, 2002). The one who holds the power of unconditional forgiveness has at his or her disposal a sovereign power (*le droit de seigneur*). The seigneur or master stands in the place of God, assuming a provisional and strategic role that is implicitly, if not explicitly, theological in nature. Unconditional forgiveness as a gift is defined as that which may be, and which perhaps can only be conferred by the state, the master, the ruler, the god of monotheisms. This gift imposes on the state a geopolitico-theological responsibility, an ethics of democratic citizenship that in principle should – and indeed Derrida would say can only be founded and grounded – on another equally unconditional state, namely hospitality. Yet, in the present, so-called democracies impose ever-increasingly restrictive and calculated models of hospitality in the names of security, safety, the rights of a sovereign nation and so forth in a time of terror; which Derrida, in a turn to Martin Heidegger, identifies as an ontotheology (discussed in Chapter 2). Hospitality is thus defined for the state ontotheologically in the name of conditional democratic citizenship, in itself a constantly shifting idea and perception of criminality that is, however, Mosaic in orientation (discussed in Chapter 3).

Whatever the circumstances demanded by the state and professional practice in criminal justice settings, hospitality is always in the gift of the practitioner in their everyday interactions and based upon an explicit acknowledgement of moral guilt. Neither Catholic theology influenced by a Roman view of the sanctity of contract and, from the 10th century, the scholastic adoption of Greek rational purity (see Chapter 3) nor Protestant understandings of justification can theorize anything more than at best an atonement (conditional forgiveness), as enshrined, for example, in the Authentic Apology Model (Allan, 2008). This approach to the forgiveness of a perpetrator of a crime or a civic offence places the onus on the wrongdoer to explain their wrongful behaviour and to accept liability; to experience an emotional response to the wrong and to action behaviour to right the wrongs done. Allan (2008), in asserting this approach, argues that criminal law and punishment are fundamental to social order and equilibrium and reinforces those processes through deterrence and offering the possibility of rehabilitation. For Allan apology is central to the process of rehabilitation by allowing the wrongdoer to humiliate themself and to show respect to victims and society and therefore demonstrate that they are not of bad character.

The secular Jewish philosopher Hannah Arendt argued that Jesus of Nazareth discovered the role of forgiveness in human affairs (Arendt, 1961), however this is challenged by Griswold (2007), who argues that she overstates the case as he finds significant evidence for concepts of forgiveness already existing in pre-Christian Greco-Roman culture. The ancient Greeks did not have a word for forgiveness; Aristotle used a range of words associated with the Greek verb *sungignosko* relating to think with, agree with, recognize; all are linked with notions of relationship and empathy (see Griswold, 2007). However, for Aristotle forgiveness is neither a virtue or religiously based but rather it is linked to civic politics (see Bash, 2015). The key is to be found in Aristotle's concept of unbearable circumstance (see Barnes, 1995), which expounds a perfectionist ethical stance tied to external forces. The virtuous, detached and rational man does not make mistakes and can be excused for events outside of his control, hence no forgiveness is required. However, importantly any sense of empathy does not extend to un–virtuous persons and the irrationality of the 'mob'. Bash (2015) highlights that within the New Testament there are differences between the Gospels and the Pauline epistles concerning the nature of forgiveness. Both Jesus of Nazareth and Paul of Tarsus challenge the link between ritual conceptions of purity, sin and forgiveness and both argue that there is an injunction on Christians to forgive. However, in the Synoptic Gospels there is an emphasis by Jesus on interpersonal forgiveness, whereby repentance is necessary to be forgiven by God, but likewise to be forgiven it is necessary to forgive others. In the following extract, the Greek verb used is *aphiemi*, which has a legal connotation of acquitting, a sense of release, to excuse and cancel a debt: 'Then Peter went up to him and said "Lord, how often must I forgive my brother if he wrongs me? As often as seven times?" Jesus answered, "Not seven I tell you, but seventy-seven times"' (Matthew 18: 21–22, New Jerusalem Bible 1130).

In contrast the point is made by Bash (2015) that Paul of Tarsus (see Chapter 4), whose epistles constitute a significant proportion of the New Testament, is not a theologian of forgiveness (he rarely mentions the word) but one of justification, and by justification he means a gift of grace to undeserving people. This is interesting because despite Paul being a Hellenized Jew, with the expectation that he would use *sungignosko*-type concepts, he actually uses the Greek *charizmoi* to express gifts of grace (Bash, 2015). In this sense, rather than the requirements of the gospels to be forgiven through forgiving, it would seem that Paul, in arguing that a justified people are a forgiven people and that even the desire to repent is as a consequence of a gift of grace, is arguing for the community to forgive as an act and expression of grace. The Pauline approach is in part a reflection of Paul's own experience (see also Breton, 1988; St Paul is discussed in detail in Chapter 4) as being complicit in murder but at no point was he asked to repent or humiliate himself before the community, neither was he required to make atonement so that the community were satisfied as to his intentions (see Pycroft and Bartollas, 2018; Pycroft, 2021a).

Forgiveness and immanent space

The hermeneutics of Jesus and Paul are the coordinates for an immanent space of possibility (see Chapter 2) which is always an invitation to offenders, victims and communities to be in a more completed (redeemed) state. The revelation of the necessity of this space is explained by Jesus of Nazareth's admonition not to judge others to avoid or break cycles of violence (see Chapter 5 for examples related to justice). In a clear statement of how to overcome mimetic violence (see Chapter 4) and to develop reciprocal relationships based in mutual giving (see Chapter 5) he says:

> Do not judge and you will not be judged; because the judgements you give are the judgements you will get, and the standard you use will be the standard used for you. Why do you notice the splinter in your brother's eye and never notice the great log in your own? And how dare you say to your brother 'Let me take that splinter out of your eye,' when look, there is a great log in your own? Hypocrite! Take the log out of your own eye first, and then you will see clearly enough to take the splinter out of your

brother's eye ... Ask, and it will be given to you; search and you will find; knock, and the door will be opened to you. Everyone who asks receives ... Is there anyone among you would hand his son a stone when he asked for bread? Or would you hand him a snake when he asked for fish? ... So always treat others as you would like them to treat you; that is the Law and the prophets. (Matthew 7: 2–5; 7–12).

The suspension of judgement and a commensurate reflection on our own complicity in violence becomes the basis for our re-reading of Judaeo-Christian texts with respect to forgiveness and redemption (Hebrew: *gā'al*), their relationship to public and private space (the law and access to material resources including obligations to outsiders); who has the right to redeem (Hebrew: *gō'ēl*, literally kinsman); the congruence between thought, feeling and action, particularly in the embracing of those who should not be embraced, namely the outsider. Central to this argument is that the Judaeo-Christian mythos deconstructs the archaic religious, which has been based upon a scapegoat mechanism against the outsider (see Chapter 4). This new approach based in *hesed* (discussed later) and grace (see Chapter 5) rather than elitist and philosophical purity universalizes love, non-violence and forgiveness.

The suspension of judgement enables us to embrace those who should not be embraced as an opening of possibilities expressed as forgiveness. This is argued by Paul in his second letter to the Corinthians: 'We will not consider anyone by human standards' (2 Corinthians 5: 16); we have been given the ministry of reconciliation through God in Christ '[r]econciling the world to himself, not holding anyone's faults against them, but entrusting to us the message of reconciliation' (2 Corinthians 5: 18–19). This reconciliation is a human responsibility modelled on God's loving kindness and forgiveness as the demonstration of both God descending and human kind's ascending (becoming divine – s the psalmist says to God about humans, '[y]ou have made them little less than gods' (Psalm 8: 5). We tend to talk about the importance of charity (*caritas* is Latin for loving kindness or charity) but according to Nygren (see Vincellete, 1998: 111) *caritas* is needs- and desire based, egocentric and acquisitive love, quid pro quo. It is self-interested in that it is intended to acquire and possess (game theory writ large). In contrast, Nygren describes *agapē* as spontaneous, unconditional, centred on God (theocentric), self-giving and self-sacrificial. *Agapē* will lead one to surrender love to another and love them purely for themself, and in Protestant theology this love is a quality of God that can only be given by Her[1] as it is beyond the capacity of humans in themselves.

In exploring redemption, the view of Paul Ricoeur is that biblical stories and texts always disrupt and reorient ordinary human understanding

(Wall, 2001). In Judaism the story of Ruth (see later) is just such an example of disruption and reorientation and contains within it key themes of redemption, and within the context of vulnerability, identity and memory. This concept of redemption is essential to understanding the development of forgiveness in the Christian-era texts, and their ideas of grace and superabundance.

This is important because the Enlightenment view based on the emerging disenchantment with religion and the reification of reason and subsequent revenge upon Christianity (reaching its apotheosis in Nietzsche) was that zealous Christianity had destroyed ancient culture and the religious harmony of the pre-Christian Roman Empire (see Whitmarsh, 2017). In her book *The Darkening Age: The Christian Destruction of the Classical World* Karen Nixey (2017) outlines the key issues that have confronted the Enlightenment and the modernist relationship with religion (the religion in question is Christianity, but Nixey also draws parallels with contemporary Islam). Her key argument is that monotheism is *always* weaponized, rather than particular examples being aberrant examples of a religious truth. We need to understand how states and communities have weaponized religion to the advantage of both themselves and the Church (and vice versa), and how this informs the development of the criminal justice system and social order. Particularly, we need to understand how Christianity, in offering a genuine epistemology of love and forgiveness, has found itself complicit in the supporting and promoting of retributive practices, including capital punishment in the processes of justice (this is discussed in Chapter 3).

As an example, within the context of the troubles in Northern Ireland and the development of a meaningful peace process the public theologian Glenn Jordan (private correspondence with Aaron Pycroft) talks about the scriptural 'clobber texts' which Churches use to justify/bolster their own positions and which have the effect of marginalizing others (see Chapter 4). For Glenn the concept of forgiveness and the New Testament texts, particularly those of St Paul, had become so weaponized that (within the context of Northern Ireland) discourse around forgiveness was not bearing fruit. There is in effect a frozen peace, with protagonists not able to move forward by giving ground, each using scripture to justify their positions. For him it was essential then to revisit the Jewish Old Testament to deepen our understanding of God's grace (see also Ganiel and Yohanis, 2019). This is in itself a really interesting inversion of how these scriptures normally are viewed, with the God of the Old Testament being associated with retribution and punishment and the God of the New Testament with forgiveness. Rather there are emergent and coherent themes, from the old to the new, which need to be read through an anthropological lens (we return to this in Chapter 4). The story of Ruth is just such an example.

The story of Ruth

The key points of the following are based around Panganiban's (2020) feminist reading of the story. It is important to remember that this is a Jewish text, of which Ruth, a non-Jew, is the protagonist, with the narrative saying nothing negative about her, her foreignness, her gender or her actions. This is despite the fact that in ancient Jewish culture Moabite women were condemned as scheming prostitutes and seducers of Jewish men. As Girard points out (see Chapter 4) it is this narration from the outsider and/or the innocent victim that is the key to understanding the uniqueness of the Judaeo-Christian tradition. This story tells of how Naomi, her husband and two sons move from Bethlehem (in Israel) to Moab (a non-Jewish country) due to famine. In Moab both sons marry Moabite women (Ruth and Orpah). During a 10-year period in Moab the husband and the two sons die, leaving Naomi a widow in a foreign land with her daughters-in-law, who have born no children. Consequently, Naomi decides to return to Bethlehem, where there has been an abundant harvest, which means that according to the ancient Israelite Law there will be special provision for the poor, widows, orphans and foreigners to glean on the fields during the harvest. Naomi tells her daughters-in-law that they would be better off returning to their own people and marrying again as Naomi could not provide for them, thus releasing them of their responsibility to go with her to Bethlehem. In the conversation Naomi conveys the Hebrew sentiment of *hesed*, which expresses a relationship between God and people grounded in loving kindness and generosity, freely given, supererogatory acts, and therefore beyond the call of duty. There is a huge literature on the meaning and implications of this word but Kynes (2010) argues that '[h]*esed* always involves an interpersonal relationship between either individuals or groups, whether that is between family members, a host, a guest, friends or a sovereign and his subjects. A degree of mutuality can be assumed since a response in kind is often expected.'

Kynes (2010) further argues that *hesed* is not an abstract idea (ideal) but always involving of practical action on behalf of another, and explicitly extended to those on the margins of society. Fishbane (2010: 152 cited by Panganiban (2020: 189) argues that 'without *hesed* we would have no world, only rules for protection; we would only have limits and limitations, not excess or self-sacrifice. Thus, the world ultimately stands on *hesed*.' *Hesed* then stands in contrast to the obligation, limitation and conditionality that are to be found in, for example, post-Enlightenment normative ethics (see Chapter 4). What the story of Ruth reveals is a story of redemption, super-abundance, and incongruous acceptance (see Chapter 4) that is unusual even within the everyday practices and context of the Jewish law.

Neither Ruth nor Orpah want to leave, in part because Naomi is old and widowed and they want to care for her, but Orpah eventually does and Naomi seeks to command Ruth to do the same and to return to her people and her gods. However, Ruth is adamant that while she is under no obligation to do so, she will stay with Naomi and care for her. Naomi acquiesces in this decision.

Importantly for Panganiban (2020), Ruth's identity and the building of her resilience in the face of grief, loss and marginalization is rooted in *hesed* and the caring for others (despite not being Jewish). A contemporary example of this is to be found in the evangelical theology of 12-step programmes (see Chapter 6), where in overcoming the person's own limitations and experiencing a spiritual awakening this message of care is taken to other people who are in the same predicament. Although not unproblematic the identity of the 'alcoholic' (see Pycroft, 2010) and redemption through mutual aid is reinforced. In the experience of both authors it is not uncommon for people to say that in this respect their addiction has been a gift to themselves as it has enabled them to become who they truly are.

On arrival in Bethlehem, the story starts to become really interesting as Naomi, to secure Ruth's future, wants to find her a husband. The harvest is good and Ruth exercises her right to glean. It is clear from the text that while the right to glean was exercised and tolerated for those on the margins of society those people were still vulnerable to insult, and physical and sexual assault. We can assume that this was more often the case when the harvest was poor (see discussions on less eligibility Chapter 4). However, Boaz, the landowner (a kinsman, discussed later), treated her favourably and ordered that she not be abused and so publicly went beyond the requirements of the Law. Ruth and Naomi benefit considerably from the amount of grain that she is able to collect, with Boaz again going beyond the requirement of the Law by allowing her to glean among the sheaves themselves and even asking his workers to pull out ears of corn for her.

What follows in the text is a remarkable scene of concealment and obscuring that is sexually charged. The space of the possibility of redemption is ambiguous as the threshing floor was often a place of prostitution. Seeing that Boaz is favouring Ruth and knowing that he is a kinsman and therefore has the right of redemption over her, Naomi hatches a plan for an 'indecent proposal' (Panganiban, 2020). She tells Ruth to wash, perfume and put on her best clothes and to go to the threshing floor, where she is to approach Boaz only after he has finished eating and drinking and is asleep so that he does not recognize her. She is to uncover his genitals (this is how sex workers of the day solicited business), lie down and wait for Boaz to tell her what to do. Boaz wakes in the night, finds a woman lying at his feet, and rather than assuming that she is a prostitute, asks her who she is. Ruth, responding to Boaz' *hesed*, is truthful that Boaz is a *gōʾēl*, a kinsman who has the right to redeem her, and invites him to cover her with his cloak and marry her, which he agrees to do.

The story does not end there. The narrative leaves unsaid whether there followed any sexual activity between Boaz and Ruth, and it is evidently not significant as Boaz agrees to talk to the elders of Bethlehem and to ask their permission to marry. What is significant is that Judaism is matrilineal and despite Ruth being a Moabite, she is accepted as a Jew through her levirate marriage, which the elders agree to. In Judaism Ruth the 'outsider' becomes not only the grandmother of King David, but then also in Christianity an ancestor of Jesus of Nazareth.

There are clear lessons here for the practices of justice. Jesus of Nazareth reveals that non-violence, forgiveness and redemption are always an option, and in this respect he universalizes the principles of *hesed*, with each and every one of us having the right to redeem. We are all called to be the *gōʾēlim* but our kinship is to give more than the bare legalistic requirement to the other.

By suspending judgement we neither deny nor confirm, in fact we suspend, the search for causality to explain how and why the person has arrived here, or where they are going (poiesis). These are secondary considerations, as first we need to accept the person as they are presenting so that we may glimpse them in themselves independently of moral guilt. Aaron Pycroft remembers welcoming service users returning to detoxification and rehabilitation programmes (whether as a criminal justice requirement or not) and saying, "It's really nice to see you again." Invariably the response was one of, "But I've failed, I've let you down." The key point was that the feelings of guilt and failure were real but in response there was no judgement, only an acceptance that the person needed the service, but the welcome was independent of any service required. It is a truly genuine welcome, indicative of forgiveness and the beginning of a redemptive relationship based on an 'equal-heartedness' (Alison, 2019) and hospitality. This is something that 12-step programmes are brilliant at, meeting people at their lowest ebb ('rock-bottom'), embracing them, and by understanding their powerlessness beginning a process of redemption; the immanent acceptance of the other is key (see Chapters 2 and 6). This compares starkly with the idea of having to be motivated before starting a programme or using coercion to seek to build motivation. In a concert in Fulsome Prison, Johnny Cash clearly articulated this when he said '[i]f I learned one thing, it's when you've hit rock bottom and have nowhere else to go, it matters that someone else cares' (Cash, 2004).

What we do in and with an encounter with the other is our choice and our responsibility, for which we are accountable to the other and others. That accountability demands to know how our actions and choices have disrupted rather than perpetuated cycles of violence and how this contributes to wisdom. This principle of self-similarity goes all the way down and mirrors the culpability of the perpetrator, the hopes of the victim and the desire of the community.

For practitioners, poiesis is the unencumbered potential of the moment and joy at prospect of a genuine encounter with the other (see Chapter 2). This is not a denial of right and wrong, but a requirement that the first encounter (a first *agapē*) precludes any judgement and is independent of any construction of sentence, risk assessment and so on. This is natality, poetic space free from all determinations, and is grounded in intuition, empathy and love (the basis of the Hebrew understanding of complicity and space).

Identity, memory and moral guilt

If forgiveness is ontologically real then likewise the theme of not forgetting (anamnesis, see Chapter 5) is found in the very origins of Judaism and is clearly linked to moral guilt as an objective reality. This is demonstrated in scriptural narratives where the key protagonists and architects of understanding of our relationship with God are scapegraces who have been redeemed (for example, King David was an adulterer and murderer, Saul was complicit in murder – see Chapter 5). According to the book of Genesis, the founder of civilization is Cain, who is not only the man who murdered his brother Abel (the brothers were the sons of Adam and Eve), but is given a mark from God to protect him from retaliatory violence, thus allowing him (and human kind) to flourish). Girard (1978) argues that all cultures have founding murders but that the real violence is concealed in myth. So, while the myth of the mark of Cain has been appropriated to justify every form of stigmatization, racism and segregation (and becomes the basis of the scapegoat mechanism which God warns us against), it is not a badge of shame but a symbol of restoration. Von Kellenbach (2013: 10) expresses it thus:

> Cain's mark is a public signifier of his guilt. It protects him and prevents the erasure of memory. There is no miraculous purification of guilt ... No sacrifice cleanses the stain of Abel's blood. No ritual absolves Cain from the guilt of the past. Instead, God's protective mark imposes radical transparency and links Cain's redemption to memory. Truth-telling becomes the basis of moral and spiritual recovery. Cain lives a successful and productive life as a married man, father and founder of a city as he grows into the memory of fratricide and (re)gains moral integrity.

Von Kellenbach (2013) cites Bonhoeffer, who argues that stupidity, blindness of heart and deliverance from evil can only be achieved by an act of grace. Grace is an external invitation, a gift (Barclay, 2015) that enables the individual to be made just again (see Chapter 5). This gift can only come from one another, rather than abdicating responsibility to an angry and demanding God, who we hope will require satisfaction for wrongs committed. Jesus makes clear that 'those whose sins you forgive they are forgiven, those whose sins you retain, they are retained' (John 20: 23).

A confrontation with real events (crimes), expressed and experienced as history and what to do about them, is part of the crisis of the ethics and practices of the criminal justice system. The writer and philosopher Jean Améry, a Jewish survivor of the Holocaust, is very clear on this (1999) need to be heard and for a calling to account. But as Primo Levi (1985) recalls, the unexpected ordinariness of the enemy you meet is disconcerting (this is what Hannah Arendt meant by the banality of evil (2006)). This then is a problem of how I phenomenologically apprehend the other, within the context of personal history, as I always come between myself and that which I perceive. Levinas sees this as a problem of solipsism and he is correct, but Girard's great insight (1978) (see Chapter 4) is that the other becomes the model for my desire and thus a source of competition and escalation to violence (see Pycroft, 2020).

My own complicity in perpetuating cycles of violence is invisible to me, as is my desire for what the other has based upon a blaming and holding to account of the other (as scapegoat) for which I feel fully justified. But the other's violence (and desire for what I have) is likewise invisible to themself. A genuine inter-subjectivity then has to accept complicity in violence, to which we are all prone, and as Pepinsky and Quinney (1991) argues, this is at the heart of criminology as peacemaking. In this complicity we are deaf, dumb and blind to everything except our own desire reflected in the face of the other. Redemption as first criminology seeks to identify and work with this complicity in everyday life, including in the workings of the criminal justice system.

What we are arguing for is less a denial of the individual's desire for retribution on the basis of the harms done to them, but rather a different mode of desire that is not structured by normative ethics. Desire which rationalizes a lack of something as the drive for that desire cannot be reconciled with the other, precisely because satisfaction is impossible. There is no like for like, only an escalation in the absence of satisfaction for the victims, hence punishment, plus fine, plus damages, plus any number of requirements on community orders.

It is stated by Julia Kristeva (1989: 13) that ' "[t]he thing" is the real that does not lend itself to signification, the center of attraction and repulsion, seat of sexuality from which the object of desire will become separated …: the Thing is an imagined sun, bright and black at the same time.' The 'Thing of crime', terrible transgressions against my person, is then the focus of my anger, and becomes '[m]y necessary thing, and absolutely my enemy, my foil, the delightful focus of my hatred … The Thing is the recipient that contains my dejecta and everything that follows from *cadere* (Latin: to fall) – it is a waste with which in my sadness I merge'. An example of this followed the Nice terrorist attacks in 2016, where residents piled garbage and spat on the place where the terrorist Mohamed Lahouaiej Bouhlel was shot dead by the police (https://www.mirror.co.uk/news/world-news/nice-terror-attack-hate-memorial-8442703).

Crime and the processes of justice that follow create unwanted and self-perpetuating relationships. This is revealed in the sentiments expressed in the UK after Police Constable Andrew Harper was killed in 2019 when he went to investigate the theft of a quad bike, which are not untypical and are therefore instructive. His feet were caught in a strap attached to a car as it sped away from the crime scene. He was dragged over a mile along the road by the speeding car and died of catastrophic injuries. The three defendants (all teenagers) were cleared of murder but convicted of manslaughter, receiving sentences ranging from 13 to 16 years. The following is taken from the statement that Andrew Harper's widow, Lissie Harper (they had only been married for four weeks) made following the trial (https://www.bbc.co.uk/news/uk-england-berkshire-53809439):

> No verdict or sentence will ever bring my incredible, selfless and heroic husband back. The results from this trial I had hoped would bring justice but in reality, make no difference to the heart wrenching pain I will continue to feel for the rest of my life. Andrew was taken from us on that horrendous night last year when his life was stolen and the lives of his family and friends altered forever. This crime whatever the outcome deliberated over in court was brutal and senseless. The way in which Andrew was robbed of his life we all know to be barbaric and inexplicable. I'm immensely disappointed with the verdict given today. Andrew served in Thames Valley Police with honour. He went out night after night risking his life for the safety and well-being of the innocent, as all police officers do with passion. Ultimately, he laid down his life for us all and it pains me more than I can ever explain that this has not been appreciated by the very people who should have seen this heroic and selfless duty, as so many other members of the public and total strangers so clearly do. Myself and Andrew's family will never come to terms with our new lives. We will never understand how such a beautiful, loving and decent human being could be dealt this fate. I now have my own life sentence to bear and believe me when I say it will be much more painful, soul destroying and treacherous journey then anyone facing a meagre number of years in prison, will experience. Myself and our families will spend the rest of our days

missing him, loving him, and being utterly proud of the incredible man that he was. We will never forget the kindness that we as a family have received from all who have supported us over the past year; friends, family, total strangers and the almighty unity of the thin blue line. From the depths of our heart thank you.

Further, Lissie Harper has written to the Prime Minister asking for a retrial that

> Andrew Harper unquestionably deserves and to see the justice system in our country as the solid ethical foundation that it rightly should be, not the joke that so many of us now view it to be. To right such a despicable wrong to our country and to keep fighting on behalf of Andrew, the future that was stolen from us and also the victims who will find themselves in this unjust situation in the future. (https://www.bbc.co.uk/news/uk-england-berkshire-53809439)

She and the Police Federation are calling for a 'Harper's Law', with mandatory life sentences for anyone who kills a serving emergency services worker while they are on duty. The UK Government announced on the 24 July 2021 that it was supporting Harper's Law and would introduce legislation as soon as possible (Ministry of Justice, 2021).

This example of where forgiveness appears to be ontologically rooted in its own impossibility (Derrida, 2002) is not untypical. We all grieve with Lissie Harper and experience her real anger towards the people who have so shattered the lives of her and her family. There is nothing abnormal in her reaction and it is admirable that she would want to use this experience to bring about change in the hope of others not experiencing what she has gone through.

The multiplicity in unity of forgiveness seeks to reconcile the singularity, the thisness (haecceity) of all concerned (see the discussion on personalism in Chapter 2), which is neither a reparation nor a satisfaction for a wrong committed. It is in this phase space of forgiveness that glimpses of the other are perceived, as sparks of intuition and empathy. Bergson (1988, 1988) argues that the past cannot be changed but its virtual dimensions can be. This is expressed by Žižek (2011: 28) as '[w]hen something radically new emerges it retroactively creates its own possibility, its own causes or conditions. A potentiality can be inserted into (or withdrawn from) past reality.' The arrow of time is central to discussions on forgiveness and redemption as the material past cannot be changed (Arendt, 1961). Moral guilt remains, the suffering is real, but the emergent (transcendent/virtual) properties inherent within complex systems (such as a therapeutic encounter) allow us to actualize a new reality because the whole is always more than the sum of its parts.

The hermeneutics of Heidegger conceive of action as being constituted by an event involving past, present and future which is not already determined, and likewise Wittgenstein argues that action is socially constituted but not socially determined (see Inwood, 2016). Action requires an apprehension and making visible of what is real, and not amnesia (see Chapter 6). In this sense, memory serves to keep what we call the past, present in the present. This appears to us as a flow of time and explains in a secular age every memorial and shrine that arises by the roadside in memorial to people killed. It also explains the naming of laws to memorialize innocent victims. They shall not be forgotten. But paradoxically in this respect every time Megan's Law, Harper's Law, Sarah's Law and so on are discussed then so is the name of the perpetrator of the crimes against them, with the victim and perpetrator locked together in perpetuity. There is no question of the innocence of the victims or the guilt of the perpetrator but these examples demonstrate also that there is no such thing as history and that the content of what we take to be in the past is very much present in the present. The traumatized constantly re-experience their trauma (see Chapter 5). So, Harper's Law (if it becomes so) invites us to remember the innocence, and virtues of Andrew Harper and what has been unjustly taken away, while at the same time inviting perpetual condemnation for those who killed him and all those like him.

This, along with justifications for other forms of penal marking, is an inversion of Judaeo-Christian thought where the potentiality of forgiveness and its actualization is to be found in an immanent affirmation of criminals, victims and communities, of what is, rather than what we hope for or wait for to emerge (see Chapter 3). We are invited to embrace the whole person, both their being and non-being (shadow). Both deontological (the forces of the past, expressed as ethics) and teleological (the forces of the future, expressed as ethics) conditionally close down this space of possibility; affirmation is expressed in the language of gift (see subsequent chapters) as a basis for this singular plural existence (Nancy, 2000). As is argued by Nancy (2000: 3), '[b]eing cannot *be* anything but being-with-one-another, circulating in the *with* and as the *with* of this singularly plural existence' (emphasis in the original).

Redemption understands our incompatibility with the other. In learning to see the nature of this incompatibility, we can address what is real and what is illusory in seeking to overcome the distance between ourselves and the other. Sartre states that '[m]an is "a being of distances"' (nd: 17), and we constantly experience 'those little pools of non-being which we encounter each instant in the depth of being' (Sartre, nd: 19). While Existentialism has no (seeks no) answer to 'annihilating nothingness', resignation or anguish, a redemptive criminology draws upon the example of Albert Camus (2000), who moves from suicide in the face of existential despair to courage and humanism. That courage is commitment and acceptance of the other and an overcoming of one's own alienation from self and the other (*méconnaissance* – see Chapter 4).

Any structured understanding of the ontological nature of forgiveness has to include non-being as an immanent rather than purely existential (apropos Heidegger and Sartre) or dialectical quality (Hegel or Marx). Tillich (1997) argues that reductionism equates non-being with empty space, and in Judaism that empty space is the domain of Azazel and sin (see Chapter 4). In this space, the disappointed expectation (no satisfaction) creates the distinction between being and non-being and it is through participation in non-being that negative judgements (leading to condemnation) are possible. Both Tillich (1997) and St Augustine agree that sin is non-being (in a Platonic sense of purity) and that sin (and by extension Satan – see Chapters 4 and 7) has no positive ontological standing; forgiveness is acceptance of the person and their moral guilt.

Through embracing non-being we can integrate, genuinely, victims, offenders and communities into mainstream justice as all experience non-being in relation to and with the other. This endeavour is not with the purpose of closing distances because after all there is now an unwanted proximity between victims and the accused/convicted, bound together through the processes of justice. This proximity causes further conflict but in seeking some form of reconciliation or healing, varying degrees of physical, emotional, psychological or environmental distance may be required. Non-being is not separate from, but constitutive of, being in the immanence of now and the totality of the situation. After all, where do lost dreams go, the good but failed intentions of not using drugs, and committing crimes? Likewise, how do victims become survivors, how are griefs and losses integrated? The non-being experienced as experiences and memories are not lost but cumulative and are the content of ongoing and often unwanted relationships.

Adversarial criminal justice effectively closes that distance through a theologically and philosophically justified violence (but which conceals the archaic sacrificial – see Chapter 4) in a constant process of proximity to the other, thus providing the process with its energy. Most victims want their day in court, want and need to be heard, but are worn down by bureaucratic process (see the discussion on Nils Christie in Chapter 4), and as Julia Kristeva (2016: 126) says in discussion with Richard Kearney, '[e]thics rarely creates joy. But loves, when we encounter them, and hates when they do not immediately destroy us, always arouse needs and desires for which we lack places and times. Experience is the single configuration by which we reach a jouissance.' An encounter between a criminal justice worker and a criminal, a victim or a community, is a proximal space to explore loves, hates and desires and a place of joy and celebration (this is something that restorative justice and structured therapeutic communities do well). This encounter of being (therapeutic) and non-being (anti-therapeutic) more often than not is the place where the worker seeks a genuine therapeutic encounter while juggling the institutional anomie and bureaucratic demands of non-being. Being seeks to express itself while non-being seeks to close down the potentiality.

Forgiveness as an expression of being is a therapeutic encounter which creates a phase space of potentiality that relates to past, present and future not as subtraction (sacrificial punishment), but as gift which in itself is an invitation to superabundance. A reintegration of the modern with the postmodern in criminology is necessary to rediscover change agency (see Milovanovic, 2019), a hermeneutical, and phenomenological approach opens up possibilities to counter the secularist failure to have a meaningful understanding of forgiveness and its centrality to addressing human social needs more generally. However, importantly, it enables us to '[s]peak again, about religion, but in a recuperative, hermeneutic mode of applying religious traditions creatively to current cultural issues' (Kearney and Zimmerman, 2016: 94). A rational interpretation of *mythos* both provides us with a structure for dealing with the aftermath of crime and opens up new lines of inquiry for developing new practices in criminal justice and human flourishing (becoming conscious in the consciousness of the other). This mythos reveals that forgiveness is authentically and ontologically human, but anthropologically social order is driven by the desire for sacrifice.

4

Apprehending the Victim

The phenomenology of Girard and also of Heidegger are read by Vattimo and Zabala (2011) as an interpretation of the meaning of history being one of emancipation from violence, but the work of Girard reveals how our own will to power in seeking to overcome that violence can undermine those efforts and ideals (how else does Heidegger become a Nazi?). It is the founding murder as the initial condition for social formation which is revealed in the Judaeo-Christian tradition. Forgiveness un-conceals this violence and offers a new social order through embracing rather than sacrificing the 'monstrous other'. This forgiveness demonstrates why the old solutions of religious sacrifice (even when dressed up in the new clothing of 'the rational') in criminal justice no longer work. Using Girard's work, we argue first that my desire to punish you is not authentic, but is a socially transmitted fantasy of regaining that which has been lost. It is group contagion linked to scapegoating mechanisms and social order based on archaic sacrifice. Second, my desire to punish you is my desire to differentiate myself from you. This differentiation spirals into an escalation of extremes, which heightens similarities rather than differences. It is this sameness which is the cause of violence. Third, that religion has controlled rather than caused mimetic violence in archaic societies through the scapegoat mechanism. This mechanism no longer works (because we know the victim is innocent) although we keep on trying to use it (this explains the punitive turn and the rhetoric of harsh sentences). The Judaeo-Christian tradition offers us the radically new resources that we need. These resources start with the individual and the need to overcome my own violence and will to power.

Post-Enlightenment philosophical influences on criminology

The critical tradition has been essential in exposing the lies and deceits of history, including the will to power of Christianity, but does not reveal radically new solutions to that violence. In this sense, its solutions are perpetually conservative and elitist; or according to Voegelin forms of Gnosticism (discussed in Chapter 2). In the dialectics of Hegel and Marx, the personal, subordinated to an impersonal and inexorable logical process (see Milbank, 2006) cannot value the individual or voluntarism. For Hegel the state is the absolute embodiment of the divine spirit. His dialectical method and the negation of the negation, whereby the conflict between a thesis and its antithesis leads to a new synthesis (identity), is we argue, problematic. The complex and emergent nature of reality (see Chapter 2) demonstrates that all complex systems are historical systems that have memory, and even the traces of that memory can influence the present in a non-linear way (it is not always clear which parts are acting on which other parts).

In the same ways that Platonic thought seeks to return to an imaginary pre-existent beginning (the article of faith for rehabilitation) and rejects poiesis, Nietzsche's eternal recurrence of the same claims the same. Nietzsche argues this as his most important thought with the idea that events in the world repeat themselves through an eternal series of cycles (Nietzsche, 2003). For Nietzsche (2003), each recurrence requires a will to power that surpasses the former affirmations of itself expressed as a master-morality that is noble, grand and virile, producing an aristocracy that challenges the slave-morality of Christian ethics. Nietzsche saw Christianity as being nothing more than the revenge of the weak against the strong and the negation of life itself. He argues for a transvaluation of values that reinstates everything the Jewish-Christian God has denounced. Nietzsche's concept of the *Übermensch* (the man who reaches over and beyond (so much so that Nancy (2000) observes Nietzsche rarely returns to earth)) clearly reinstates an aristocracy based on inequality and thus the violence of the strong against the weak.

The work of Nietzsche, Marx and Freud in exposing the lies of modernity and pointing out religion's own will to power and complicity in violence has been essential but their solutions do not break with, but rather perpetuate, those cycles of violence. Therefore, each theorist in their own way embraces and feels justified in their violence (or does not see it as violence – see later for a discussion of *méconnaissance*) and this is, we argue, problematic for the critical tradition in criminology. It was observed by Albert Camus (2000) that you cannot be a 'part time nihilist', and this is, we argue, the position that much critical criminology finds itself in through at best an unconscious acceptance of violence through an unquestioning acceptance of philosophical resources. For Voegelin a feature of Gnosticism is the closing down of questioning and Camus argued that the pro-communist members of the French existential movement ignored Stalin's atrocities. In his *Critique of Dialectical Reason* (Sartre, 1976) Sartre's treatment of existential philosophy in combination with Marxism approves of collective murder and 'fraternity terror'.

In understanding nihilism, the particular influence of the Marquis de Sade in this genealogy needs addressing in criminology. In his claim for absolute freedom, including from the 'purity' of Christianity (as grounded in Greek thought), he committed acts of sexual violence. He was an elected delegate to the National Assembly after the French Revolution and was asked to join the judiciary, however he refused on the basis that '[h]e would only kill for pleasure and not for justice' (Wainhouse and Seaver, 1966: xi). The influence of de Sade's writings was influential on Nietzsche and his repudiation of Christian weakness and its slave mentality. In the same way that Nietzsche's elitism is disregarded in favour of his rehabilitation as an existential philosopher (Cotkin, 2005), Wernick (1982:182–3) states:

> In an extraordinary reversal, de Sade, whose writings have been excoriated for two centuries as 'dirty, dangerous, violent', has been gradually disinterred by radical intellectuals and made the subject of increasingly sympathetic re-evaluation. Indeed, since the lifting of the ban on his work in the '50s and '60s, the Divine Marquess has not only become established as a polite topic of intellectual conversation, but he has been virtually rehabilitated as an ideological figure ... In the eyes of critical theory de Sade disclosed the erotic telos of dominated reason: Belsen in the bedroom. At this pedagogical level, and despite himself, de Sade has positive value as an honest and illuminating spokesman for Enlightenment rationality: closer in truth-value if not in piety to the liberal–rationalist tradition that hypocritically silenced him and whose authentic representative he nevertheless really was.

Similarly, we find that Miller (1990: 471) argues that '[t]his strange double transvaluation' applies when reading Foucault's *Discipline and Punish* (1977). In the original French *Surveiller et Punir*, *Surveiller* (to watch, or control and to be caught up in the spectacle) is much closer to Foucault's meaning than the translation in English of 'discipline' in his promoting both scepticism concerning judicial reforms to reduce pain and suffering and yet simultaneously revealing a fascination for the institutions that promote visible displays of cruelty and sadism. Miller proposes that this implicit cruelty is too challenging to contemplate in most philosophies, and we extend this argument to suggest that the challenge is precisely in acknowledging our own unconscious complicity in violence and scapegoating as the default position of human society, which prides itself on rationality and 'evidence-based approaches' to rehabilitation. As Girard (1978) argues, we can always identify those scapegoated but we cannot identify our own scapegoating processes, against innocent people, as we feel justified in our violence (see later). Miller (1990: 485) summarizes the work of Nietzsche and Foucault as, to be truly human, cruelty is better externalized than internalized, better to be active than weak and reactive, and to bear witness to 'the continuing chaos of instinctive violence'.

In addition, the genealogy from de Sade-Nietzsche to Foucault is mediated by that of Heidegger. While Heidegger presents us with a radical interpretation of truth, and becoming conscious of what is hidden through discovering what we value, then he too falls foul of the scapegoating process through a gnostically inspired immenentization of the eschaton (discussed in Chapter 2). His Nazism and anti-Semitism have come to the fore in the publication of his Black Notebooks (see Mitchell and Trawney, 2017). Ultimately, he argued in his interview with *Der Spiegel* (Sheenan 2017) (only allowed by him to be published posthumously) 'that only a God can save us now' (back to the question of which God and how are they to be named?).

Throughout this genealogy we find an ongoing fragmentation through reduction to complicit violence based on the Dionysian (Nietzschean) principle of accepting the suffering of the innocent. In the name of the greater good, every individual has the potential for being dispensed, sacrificed or traded off. At best, the apotheosis of Nietzsche's *Übermensch* is Foucault's commitment to sado-masochism in both his thought and private life (see Miller, 1993). The risk here is a sexualization of punishment where a plateau, a quivering intensity, an orgasm without release (Massumi, 1996) simply seeks to carry the pleasure forward at the expense of others but with no resolution to the pain and a diminishment of pleasure.

Girard and an anthropology of the cross

In contrast in the Judaeo-Christian scriptures which were so despised by this genealogy, we find the potential for loving and entering into the pain of every individual with practices based on inclusion rather than exclusion, in excess and superabundance rather than exclusion and reduction to violence (even to the self). This is not a Platonic or idealized tradition but one that demands anthropic responsibility to the flesh, blood and welfare of people, as expressed in the Christian Eucharistic meal (see Chapter 7), rather than seeking to soar beyond reality. The distinctive message of Judaeo-Christianity heralds the end of sacrificial violence rather than its justification (see Gorringe, 1996) as foundational to a radical proclamation of equality before God and people (see Chapter 5). The Girardian analysis is a hermeneutic of suspicion which when applied to the criminal justice system reveals the nature of the archaic and sacred sacrificial within that context. Girard further reveals that Christianity, technically, is not a religion (in the archaic sense) but an organizing and generative principle that deconstructs the archaic religious through revealing the function of sacrifice to social order. Further, it provides a hermeneutic of affirmation and ways to move beyond that violence.

However, paradoxically (unwittingly, unconsciously?) the Nietzschean genealogy actually reveals the truth of this gospel message, as being uniquely written from the perspective of innocent victims who engage in radical forgiveness that is, it is written by those who have been scapegoated. This was the initial inspiration for Rene Girard (2008) and argued by Alison (2003) that where Girard and Nietzsche meet then theology is forged. This understanding informs our criminological argument. At the fault line between Nietzsche and Girard we see both violence and forgiveness as embodied and intertwined, but with a way out of that violence, contra Nietzsche, Heidegger and Foucault. Neither is there a resort to simplistic *deus ex machina* solutions. Neither is it an idealist, dialectical or utilitarian process, but emergent, requiring an immanent response based upon a hermeneutic of affirmation. Criminal justice seeks to reduce the divine to the measure of man (see Marion, 2012) and so the practices of rehabilitation in criminal justice are designed to fail because its success would be too demanding and require a reordering of our social, economic and political relationships. The hermeneutic key to understanding this failure is to be found in the Judaeo-Christian scriptures, which reveal both our irrational scapegoating (unconsciousness), our capacity to become conscious (rational) and a realization that time (expressed as teleology and eschatology) is an illusion that promotes violence based on metaphysics and an abdication of our own responsibility. Theologically and anthropologically, this is both the actions of the community on behalf of that community and all of its constituent members engaging with radical and unconditional grace. This acceptance in the Christian mythos is one of paradox (see Milband, 2006). The torture, execution and resurrection of Jesus of Nazareth is an embracing of life and death that does not require a dialectical resolution. In Bohm's quantum mechanics (see Chapter 2) it is an example of the flow of undivided wholeness, which avoids the risk of collapse into either Platonic, decontextualized metaphysics based on notions of purity, or self-defeating violence towards the other, a philosophy of creativity that is not entropic in nature.

All institutions, including modern justice systems, have founding myths, which evolve over time. Historical practice has woven together the exercise of utilitarian power (myths of rationality and social contract giving rise to concepts of less eligibility and risk assessment) alongside the explicitly theological language of rehabilitation (metaphysical judgement, the virtues of hope and making good focusing on developing pro-social attitudes to justify access to social and human capital). As Hathaway (2003) argues, it is impossible to understand the law as it is practised now without understanding the law as it has been practised in the past. Hathaway, in examining the role of history in law, highlights the importance of tradition in constitutional interpretation, the role of historical narrative in decision making and the value of precedent. With respect to the practices of criminal justice we argue that an overt focus on retribution and punishment is not the only possible outcome from history, but we need to understand how this path lock has emerged and how it can be shifted. To understand this path lock and its antecedents we need to examine the relationship between theology and law and the alternate possibilities that the Judaeo-Christian tradition offers us.

Girard and mimetic theory

In developing both an evolutionary theory of culture (genetic and social), Girard identifies a phenomenology of mimesis that is inter-individual, social and generative in nature. Girard's argument that the Judaeo-Christian scriptures reveal the sacrificial victim mechanism that is at the heart of all human culture has been highly influential across a range of disciplines, but not criminology. This despite Girard's being a radical victimology that literally deifies the victim and helps us to understand our own unconscious complicity in violence. To some degree, it would appear that these unconscious drives negate the possibility of escaping violence, and thus Girard's worldview is apocalyptic. Therefore, while Girard's thought has been utilized as a hermeneutic of suspicion in the humanities and social science, within those disciplines little attention is paid to the solutions to these problems that he suggests. That is because he argues for a personalist ethics grounded in *imitatio Dei* (see Jun, 2007). Not only does this approach appear to challenge the very foundations of liberal democracy, its claims to rationality and separation from myth, but it also undermines the claims of dominant scholastic theology with respect to atonement (see later) and its justifications for retributive practices. The question is which God we want to imitate, and whether we want to imitate the Judaeo-Christian God, who appears angry and vengeful and who cannot be a resource in restorative justice, for example (Johnstone and Ness, 2007).

In addressing these questions, Girard reveals much of what the Christian narrative obscures. In the words of Richard Kearney (1999: 252):

> Girard seeks accordingly to make the operations of our social imaginary – i.e. our ideological unconscious – answerable to ethics. He resolves to subject ideologies of scapegoating to critical hermeneutics of suspicion, exposing concealed meanings behind apparent ones ... sacrificial figures though invariably aliens and excoriated by their contemporaries become hallowed over the ages until they are eventually remembered as saviour gods who restored their community from chaos to order. They emerge out of the mists of time as miraculous 'others' who managed to transmute conflict into law. But this miraculous alteration of sacrificed 'aliens' into sacred 'others' is predicated upon a strategic forgetfulness of their original stigmatisation.

The mimetic mechanism (see, for example, Girard, 1978; Girard, 2007) is a generative process, the evidence for which can be found in myths of all kinds from around the world, but is particularly revealed in the Judaeo-Christian mythos. It covers a process that begins with mimetic desire, leading to mimetic rivalry, escalating to mimetic conflict and ends with the scapegoat resolution. Girard differentiates between desire and appetites with basic needs for biological survival not connected with desire. The latter is mimetic (imitative) and brought about by the presence of a model which is the key to his whole theory. Through mimesis, the subject will desire the same object possessed or desired by that model. The consequences of that desire are largely determined by proximity to that model, for example I want what my celebrity hero has but we live in very different worlds and so a direct conflict between the two of us is not very likely as the objects of my model are beyond my reach. This is an externally mediated relationship. However, if my model is someone in my domain then their objects are accessible to me and this mimetic relationship is powerfully reinforcing (internally mediated) as both people imitate each other and become symmetrical doubles with an intense rivalry. The focus becomes the defeat of the other rather than the object itself, with the doubles becoming identical and undifferentiated: 'A mimetic crisis is always a crisis of undifferentiation that erupts when the roles of subject and model are reduced to that of rivals. It's the disappearance of the object which makes it possible. This crisis not only escalates between the contenders, but it becomes contagious with bystanders' (Girard, 2007: 57).

In criminal justice, Nils Christie (1977) identifies the problem of undifferentiation in his conflicts as property argument. Christie (1977: 1) argues that his 'suspicion is that criminology to some extent has amplified a process where conflicts have been taken away from the parties directly involved and thereby have either disappeared or become other people's property. In both cases a deplorable outcome.' Christie argues for the importance of individuals owning their conflicts as a source of creativity rather than having them stolen by the depersonalizing forces of the state in the form of lawyers and treatment professionals.

This depersonalization is another form of fragmentation and disjunction (see Chapter 2) designed to resolve conflict in the name of a greater good by those professionals. With regard to treatment personnel, he argues that their function is to convert 'the image of the case from one of conflict into one of non-conflict' (Christie, 1977: 4), with the non-conflict perspective being a precondition for defining crime as a legitimate target for treatment. In both the legal and treatment settings there is increased specialization, bureaucratization and hence the development of trained incapacity. Building upon the work of Thorstein Veblen, the philosopher Kenneth Burke (Burke, 1954) developed the concept of trained incapacity, which refers to situations whereby one's abilities actually function as blindness. Burke (1954: 7) gives the example of businesspeople '[w]ho through long training in competitive finance, have so built their scheme of orientation about this kind of effort and ambition that they cannot see serious possibilities in any other system of production and distribution'.

In discussing trained incapacity Burke (1954) also make a linkage with mechanisms of scapegoating, which is very similar to Girard's work (see Pycroft, 2019). Both of these thinkers identify the ways in which a scapegoat becomes a useful resolution to a crisis that is, we can blame someone for the problem and transfer our anger onto them. For Burke this is a developing occupational psychosis brought about by routinization (automatic behaviour); for Girard it is always unconscious.

The Girardian reading of Christie's thesis is that the crime is no longer the object of rivalry. In fact this disappears as the professionalized processes of the court take dominance (seek to externally mediate). With the lack of real resolution everybody is left dissatisfied through the processes of undifferentiation, which lead to conflict in an escalation to extremes brought about by the court's inability to satisfy any of the stakeholders. This leads to a process whereby the other becomes a focus of anger, seen as justified and blamed for the failures of the external mediation and which in modern settings is often played out through the media and social media, with people taking sides against one other.

Scapegoat rituals

Girard argues (1978; 2007 that scapegoat rituals are the process by which violence is contained and resolved in societies and is the basis of religious rituals. Girard identifies the scapegoat mechanism as being behind every ritual including those of justice, punishment and denunciation (Girard, 1978). Likewise, Dupuy (2013) observes that with the decline of the twin pillars of religion and monarchy justice is the only publicly ubiquitous ritual that advanced industrial countries have left. Girard (1978) argues that the scapegoat is a coherent enough interpretation of all rituals that resemble the Leviticus ritual. In the Mosaic ritual of the Day of Atonement (Leviticus 16) the scapegoat is that one of the two goats chosen by lot to be sent alive into the wilderness, the sins of the people having been symbolically laid upon it, while the other was appointed to be sacrificed. Whether physical or psychological, the violence directed at the victim appears to be justified because the scapegoated person has brought about some evil that must be avenged, resisted and oppressed. History and contemporaneous societies are replete with examples, and in addressing mimetic violence and social disorder the scapegoat restores order through becoming the focus for retribution and denunciation. An unconscious dimension is always present in the social order as a process of displacement or transference from the persecutors who are the majority towards their victims who are a minority. This is clearly expressed by Jesus, who, during his crucifixion, stated, 'Father forgive them, they do not know what they are doing' (Luke 23: 34); likewise, as he is being stoned to death, Stephen 'knelt down and said aloud, "Lord do not hold this sin against them"' (Acts 7: 60). Girard (2014) argues that in scapegoating the victim is always innocent in the face of the violent collective, and that Christianity has taken the side of innocent victims. The judicial execution of Jesus of Nazareth demonstrates this given that he was innocent but was the chosen scapegoat to restore social order in Jerusalem at a time of violent unrest. Nietzsche, for example, sees this as nothing more than revenge by the weak against the strong; a Christian slave mentality indicated by forgiveness, which in itself was nothing more than a form of revenge (Nietzsche, 2003).

Christianity's will to power

The question central to the Christian mythos is why or whether Christ had to die, and there is no settled agreement in Christianity regarding this question. Hanson and Hanson (1985) argue that because the early Christian Church was a living contemporary atonement– forgiving sins, reconciling, healing – it was not necessary to do theology about it. However, the theological debates and teachings over time concerning the nature of Christ's death and the reasons for it have had a fundamental impact on shaping attitudes to punishment and atonement in the development of modern states and are an example of the Church's own will to power and its *méconnaissance* (see later). The seeds of this will to power are to be found in the controversy over the words that Jesus spoke on the cross and whether he said 'Father, forgive them for they do not know what they are doing' (Luke, 23: 34). This is discussed in Chapter 5.

Prior to Anselm of Canterbury (1033–1109) a Christus Victor theology saw mankind as being in bondage and held hostage to the evil powers of Sin, Death and the Devil. This is not dissimilar to Aristotle's idea of unbearable circumstances (that is, the virtuous man did not need forgiveness because any wrong done could only be due to external circumstances beyond his control), however under this human (anthropological)-focused theology (see Eddy and Beilby, 2006) Christ frees mankind from those circumstances irrespective of their purity or rationality (Aulen, 2010). Aulen (2010) argues that this theology was rich in imagery and metaphor but was displaced by a more 'rational' approach based on satisfaction theory. Satisfaction theory is Godward looking (Eddy and Beilby, 2006) and argues that the justification for punishment and retribution is that God himself is punitive and demands satisfaction through sacrifice and punishment for every sin so as to make atonement. These fundamental changes (bifurcation) in theological thinking coincide with the rediscovery of Greek philosophy by Islamic and Christian scholastics; hence, the Aristotelian influence of purity and elitism becomes apparent.

This idea, reinforced by Augustine's earlier Platonic ideas in the City of God (Augustine, 1958) is that the state is a bulwark against sin. In this historical development and in seeking to understand why liberal democracies that have had a Christian identity are so punitive in their approaches to criminal justice, contra biblical accounts of forgiveness Gorringe (1996) argues that religion and law are related at the deepest level and that

> Christian theology constituted the most potent form of ideology in western society for at least a thousand years up to the 18th/19th centuries and its ideological importance is by no means dead. It was both influenced by, and influenced, penal thinking. It represented a construal of the crucifixion of Christ, by no means inevitable, which reinforced retributive thinking, according to which sin or crimes have to be punished and cannot be dealt with in any other way.

Gorringe argues that satisfaction theory emerged in the 11th century at the same time as criminal law took shape and they reacted on each other, with theology drawing on legal notions and law looking for metaphysical justification. The contrast between the two approaches is significant as in satisfaction theory Christ is the only acceptable sacrifice to an angry God who demands retribution, whereas Christus Victor is a freely given act of love from God, in the face of unbearable circumstances for mankind, for example '[t]he gift of grace expressed in the Pauline letters, and the cross of Christ is not a justification of punishment but a heralding of its end' (Gorringe, 1996: 269).

The rediscovery of Greek philosophy by the medieval scholastics may have provided a framework for establishing a purely rational theology but in so doing discarded the dramatic symbolism of classical atonement. Thus, perhaps unwittingly, a theology of purity and individualization reinstated a Greek view of unbearable circumstances alongside Christian notions of sin, penance and satisfaction negating the Biblical view of the powerlessness of Everyman and the need for outside and freely given help (grace).

This philosophically informed approach to theology has been essential to the creation of a hegemonic and state-sponsored Christian religion, fundamental to social order and therefore complicit in cruelty, punishment and the exercise of power. It is argued by Martin (2014: 42) that

> [i]t is not in the least surprising that Christianity devised strategies of negotiation, compromise and assimilation as it spread in societies characterised by discourses of power and codes of honour. On the contrary, the history of Christianity ... follows precisely the course you would expect ... the presentation of Christianity was often loaded towards the Old Testament, so that rulers fashioned their self-understanding in the image of Solomon, David, Hezekiah

or Josiah. Appropriations of the figure of Christ crucified by monarchs and ecclesiastics were much less popular because less plausible and persuasive, except when deployed at tangents that ignored the stripping away of the human dignity of Christ by the legally constituted authorities in 'Church' and state. The Godly Prince of the Renaissance ruling jure divino found scant gratification in the role of a convicted felon.

Méconnaissance

In his psychoanalytically informed argument that scapegoating should not be seen as a conscious activity based on a conscious choice, Girard argues that the process is effective precisely because there is an element of delusion to which we are all susceptible. This means that all of us can condemn examples of scapegoating yet none of us can identify our own involvement in it. This is an example of what Girard identifies as *méconnaissance*, which in the French language can relate to a mistake, false information, illusion, misrecognition or mis-cognition, but for which in the English there is no adequate and single definition. Within this argument, it is through *méconnaissance* that the self-organizing and self-regulating process of violence, which is foundational to the origins of human culture and institutions, remains hidden. Girard argues that Christian revelation lifts the veil of *méconnaissance* so that we now understand the innocence of the scapegoat, and that its presumed guilt has protected us from understanding our own violence. The consequences of this knowledge are that the scapegoating mechanism and the institutions built upon it become less effective (this is the basis of the disenchantment with religion in modernity) and leaving us with the problem of how to effectively deal with mimetic crises given the innocence of the other.

A reduction in *méconnaissance* invites a new perspective on the innocence of scapegoats and our own complicity in violence, which can instigate a new space of possibility. Dumouchel (2011: 105) argues:

> [T]he revelation that is necessary in order to make unanimous victimage impossible is something that will help dissolve individual méconnaissance, something that will make less likely both the actions and representations that come with it. This ... is not so much the revelation of the innocence of the victim, as the revelation of the innocence of the other, which is not so much the revelation of the 'sanctity' of the other, as the revelation of his or her radical and fragile humanity. What destroys this méconnaissance is not a belief, a propositional content, but new attitudes like forgiveness and charity extended to all.

The satisfaction theory of atonement saw a re-emergent *méconnaissance* through a restatement of philosophical rather than biblical principles, which justified human violence modelled on God's (perceived) violence. The sacred sacrificial as the basis of the modern state was legitimated through theology and provided an infinite resource of metaphysical justifications for harsh punishments, meaning that individuals become locked into the criminal justice system. This lock-in means that people are provided with a teleological promise of reward after they have 'made good' but are not provided with the resources to enable them to do this as more sacrifice not less is required to give satisfaction.

Criminal justice as the sacred sacrificial

The criminal justice system is the place of the sacred sacrificial and largely unaffected by processes of secularization. This could reflect Nietzsche's (2003: 14) argument that

> God is dead. God remains dead. And we have killed him. How shall we comfort ourselves, the murderers of all murderers? What was holiest and mightiest of all that the world has yet owned has bled to death under our knives: who will wipe this blood off us? What water is there for us to clean ourselves? What festivals of atonement, what sacred games shall we have to invent? Is not the greatness of this deed too great for us? Must we ourselves not become gods simply to appear worthy of it?

However, interestingly, Camus (2000) argued that Nietzsche did not kill God but found him already dead in the hearts of his contemporaries and therefore, on this basis, had to act. The Girardian view is that this action and its 'will to power' served the purpose of preserving the scapegoat and an elitist aristocracy over and above the radical equality of the Christian gospel. This closes down the space of potentiality as it is still acceptable for an innocent victim to suffer in meeting the needs of the community.

With respect to both Church and state and their respective wills to power it would appear that each has become the model for the other's desire, leading to their imitating each other in seeking metaphysical justification for violence and power (see Gorringe, 1996). As argued by Eugene Webb (1988: 183) for Girard '[c]onsciousness is something that must be struggled for and won from the unconscious', and hermeneutics help us to examine the relationships between ideology and religion and the ways in which an '[i]deological recollection of sacred foundational acts has the purpose ... of integrating and justifying a social order' (Kearney, 1986: 112). This helps us to address the question of how in societies whose cultural identity is rooted in the Judaeo-Christian tradition we have moved from (at least the potential for) radical, creative and radically reinforcing stories of forgiveness and grace to those of a dominant narrative of conditionality and punishment.

Our argument, like Nietzsche's, is one of anthropic responsibility, and rather than abdicating that responsibility to an angry and vengeful God, we find our argument supported by the very gospel that Nietzsche rejects. In satisfaction theories of atonement through the 'rediscovery' of Greek thought and its elitism based on purity, the sacrifice of Christ is transvaluated and thus the understanding of the nature of God is changed. This approach cannot apprehend what is truly human (solidarity born out of powerlessness) and neither will Nietzsche's haughtiness tolerate that weakness. Only the Christian tradition offers a genuine anthropology that affirms people as they are, rather than as they might be. Nietzsche provides us with a transvaluation of suffering, and a justification of teleological violence based on sacrificing the innocent in the name of a people yet to be. Thus, Nietzsche and all systems of metaphysics do not return us to earth and do not truly affirm the flesh and blood of our common humanity. A re-reading of the Jewish rite of Atonement (see later) provides us with this affirmation, with a phase space that is not Platonic but dynamic, where heaven and earth meet, and an implicate order rejects mechanized matter. A phenomenological apprehension of reality reveals both the haecceity and individuation of the parts (victim, criminal, community members) of the system and affirms their ontological connectedness contra Nietzschean self-sufficiency. The scapegoat mechanism transvaluates innocent victims into gods, and acts to conceal this creative violence, but the biblical basis of atonement transubstantiates matter (see Chapter 7), consciousness and time into a new reality that acknowledges both memory and becoming as constituent of being.

For Marion (2012), God is beyond being and is free in all determinations (aseity) and the failure of metaphysics is precisely to ascribe categories of being to 'Him' (see Baker and Whitehead, 2020 for research findings that link a masculine view of God with harsh criminal punishment and militarism). He argues that Nietzsche not only reveals the death of the metaphysical God, but under Her various conceptual names metaphysical idols are imposed on a God who has yet to be encountered. Marion is, then, arguing for the death of a certain kind of God, namely the God of metaphysics. This god of punishment has become the idol of the criminal justice system in all its justifications. Marion, then, calls God by the most theological of names 'Charity', with the revelation of *agapē* belonging to neither premodernity, postmodernity nor modernity.

Aseity

At the heart of this argument is the difference between aseity and *ab alio*. In the Christian doctrine of the Holy Trinity (Father, Son and Holy Spirit) each is the model for the other and, where there is no competition and rivalry, giving entirely of the self to the other without loss of identity, meaning or purpose. Identity, meaning and purpose are endlessly created anew. It is only through acknowledging the necessity of the existence of a God without being that we do not create Her in our own image by ascribing metaphysical characteristics and Marion (2012) argues that God needs to be released from this ontotheology. A consequence of this metaphysic following Anselm through Aquinas is that in responding to evil then revenge becomes the only remedy, with

> [t]he height of evil (consisting) in perpetuating evil with the intent of suppressing suffering, in rendering others guilty in order to guarantee one's own innocence. For the more I want to assure my innocence – as is quite natural! – the more I discharge my sufferings and my responsibilities on someone else, in short the more I engulf him in evil. (Marion, 2002: 8)

Jesus has no model except the Father, whose existence is one of aseity rather than *ab alio*, with the latter referring to beings receiving their existence from others. With respect to culture, mimetic desire is *ab alio* as the other is taken as a model in determining the object of desire. De Castro Rocha (https://arcade.stanford.edu/blogs/mimetic-theory-and-latin-america) refers

> specifically to Girard's notion of 'ontological sickness' (in French, 'mal ontologique'). That is, the fact that the self cannot but depend upon others in the determination of his 'own' desire. As a necessary corollary of this assumption, the self is defined by a fundamental instability, which paradoxically reinforces the dependence upon others.

Méconnaissance means that we do not see things clearly due to the contingent nature of reality, similar to Martin Luther's argument that the revelation of God is always indirect and concealed. We do not apprehend this revelation through philosophical principles but through scripture alone (*sola scriptura*). Clearly, the Girardian view elevates the Judaeo-Christian mythos as articulated in scripture to a universal level but through the lens of modern modes of inquiry and scholarship.

It is the desiring of what the other has that becomes metaphysical violence and ontological sickness. The solution of Jesus is horizontal (giving to the other person – see Chapter 5) rather than the judicial appeal to the vertical (the God of metaphysics) because he understood the mimetic spiral that exponentially doubles interpersonal violence with the involvement of more people. The only solution then is the scapegoat mechanism, bringing temporary respite. In criminal justice, the intention of appealing to the metaphysical is to adjudicate between individuals but, as argued earlier, the processes increase similarities between the victim, the perpetrator and communities, thus exacerbating violence. These processes become dissipative structures, which are where complex dynamics are caused by irreversible processes. These structures, identified by Ilya Prigogine and Lefever (1973), are central to understanding the thermodynamics of the entropic universe and the decay associated with the arrow of time, however in contrast the immanent condition allows for a 'mutual presence, the second person, the *thou* or the *you*, (which) is the presupposition of every distinctively personal relation' (Staal, 2008: 37). The learning to see returns us to that which is whole (hale, holy) and existing in the now rather than dissipation. Staal (2008: 37) argues:

> All theories that claim to explain the causation of human action end up abstracting from the personal reason of the thinker. This is keenly true of different types of relativism and reductionism, which claim a present-company-excepted clause that grants them an epistemological status they would deny to others. 'Mystery' … denotes those experiences that defy explanation in terms of those instrumental reason or natural causation. Foremost among these are the realities of personal identity and human agency, including thinking.

For Girard all desire is a desire for being contra non-being, and my desire to punish the other and even my desire for punishment is mimetic. A clear articulation of this mimesis is in the ancient Babylonian and Mosaic traditions of 'an eye for an eye …', with the implication of proportionality and limits to punishment. What Jesus understood was that this mimesis becomes acquisitive and leads to violence:

> You have heard how it was said: *Eye for eye and tooth for tooth.* But I say this to you: Offer no resistance to the wicked. On the contrary, if anyone hits you on the right cheek, offer him the other as well; if someone wishes to go to law with you to get your tunic, let him have your cloak as well. And if anyone asks you to go one mile go two miles with him. Give to anyone who asks you, and if anyone wants to borrow, do not turn away. You have heard how it was said; *You will love your neighbour* and hate your enemy. But I say this to you, love your enemies and pray for those who persecute you; so that you may be the children of your Father in heaven, for he causes his sun to rise on the bad as well as the good. (Matthew 5: 38–45)

5

Gifting Repentance

The lack of differentiation in the processes of criminal justice leads to a permanent crisis, and escalation to extremes as defined by acquisitive mimesis and exacerbated by utilitarian approaches to rehabilitation. The work of Merleau-Ponty (1968) provides us with an opportunity to understand the single fundamental phenomenon of flesh (Fr: *la chair* derived from Lat: *cathedra*; Gr: *kathédra*) and the embodiment of difference in the Christian tradition. For him life is *la chair*, of which we are all a part, where 'the sentient being is embedded within an indivisible whole, an insurpassable specular being, a visibility and tangible in itself' (Voss, 2013: 122). Merleau-Ponty (1968) extends the argument about flesh and touch to seeing and develops his thought in tandem with modern art. He argues that science is concerned with explaining rather than seeing (see Chapter 2) and likewise philosophy treats seeing as a mode or variant of thinking. Christianity as biblical hermeneutics reveals a radical alterity through the embodiment (*la chair*) of difference (the body of Christ). For us this leads to actual peace and social cohesion through breaking the link between ritual purity and sin. Jesus, in conversation with the Pharisees, inverts the creation myth of Judaism to place difference (alterity) at the beginning (*arche*) on the first day of creation (see Falque, 2015). The first chapter of the Book of Genesis says that on the first day God created the heavens and the earth, and then only on the sixth day did he create male and female; whereas Jesus says (Matthew 19:4) '[f]rom the beginning of creation, God made them male and female'. Thus, difference is ontologically a part of creation, intended to exist, and is the basis for forgiveness, repentance and redemption through an embodiment of that difference. This alterity focuses on the stranger and even the monstrous other, which resides in every person. As Richard Kearney (2010: 152) states:

> If the sacred stranger were identical with the self, she would be neither sacred nor strange. The stranger is sacred in that she always embodies something *else*, something *more*, something *other* than what the self can grasp or contain ... From ... biblical and Greek inaugurations, the stranger is recognised as the one who can make the impossible possible, who brings sameness and alterity into fertile congress. (emphases in the original)

The revelation of this dynamical space of the embodiment of difference is a meal, shared and motivated by equal-heartedness between God and humanity. The 'Eucharist of the everyday' (Kearney, 2010: 153), actualizes the virtual thought and word into an embodied flesh that acts and engages the other. This embodiment of things is where the dynamics of the system actualize need rather than desire, delimited by the horizon of identity (that is, there are infinitely new possibilities – see Chapter 2) an immanent connection between things. In phenomenology the content of the phenomena cannot be exhausted so how much more so the interconnectedness of phenomena? Things are connected rather than isolated, which is the explanation for change; further energy and matter are the same things but differentiated by their stages of transformation (see Hodder, 2012 and Chapter 2). The shift from violent and acquisitive mimesis breaks the fantasy of justified violence and the desire for individual satisfaction. According to Alberto Manguel (2018):

> Imagining retaliation is essentially making up gratifying stories and in such scenarios some justice can be seen to be done. Satisfaction comes from the intellectual understanding of not allowing evil to go on unmarked. Pardon releases the offended from nurturing the offence in the mind. Jane Eyre forgives her evil guardian Mrs Reid as without her pardon the chapter cannot end and a new one begin.

To begin a new chapter (phase space) of life following crime, whether as a victim or perpetrator, we need a window into the lives of the other rather than ethical constructs that simply mirror our own desire. Forgiveness provides this window and an understanding that potential for redemption is contained within the transgression, a truth revealed through storytelling rather than metaphysical models of theology or philosophical ethics.[1] Embracing both the being and non-being of the person, the potential for redemption (see Chapter 6) is contained within the transgression, and through hermeneutics the subject is always in the story (whether as victim or criminal), a speaking/spoken subject who is seeking the meaning of their experience as reader/writer of their life and creating their identity (see Kasza, 2016). These stories (including myths) have the power to disrupt our perceptions of justice, retribution and forgiveness.

In Pycroft and Bartollas (2018) we provide examples of such stories, including those of Terri Roberts and Eva Kor. Terri Roberts (Roberts with Windle, 2015) tells the story of her Son Charlie Roberts and his shooting of 10 Amish girls in a schoolhouse in Pennsylvania in 2006. Five girls were murdered, the others seriously injured, and then he killed himself. Immediately following the shooting, the Amish Bishop extended forgiveness to the killer. What is remarkable about this account is the ways in which the Amish community, including the parents of the killed and injured children, reached out to Terri Roberts and her family despite the pain, anguish and grief that they were feeling. Over time, it became possible to establish solid relationships with both parents, other members of the community and the surviving children. There is one example from the book that both practically and symbolically represents the movement of the injured individuals and the community towards the perpetrator and his family: Charlie Roberts himself was to be buried with a quiet service in a cemetery away from the town in which he lived and the massacre occurred. The Police assured the Roberts family of complete privacy and no press intrusion. However, as they arrived at the cemetery the media were present in large numbers but unbeknown to the family the Amish community were also there and they surrounded and shielded the family from the media intrusion.

Oscar Groning was an SS Guard at Auschwitz who kept records of the belongings that were confiscated from the prisoners on entry to the camp. Groning had never denied his guilt but was tried due to a change in the law that allowed for his prosecution. During the trial Eva Kor, who was a prisoner in Auschwitz and, along with Miriam her twin sister, was experimented on by Josef Mengele, publicly forgave Groning. After giving her testimony, she walked across the courtroom, shook his hand and embraced him. Afterwards she said that the reason for this unplanned action was that 'I wanted to thank him for having some human decency in accepting responsibility for what he has done. I was always interested in meeting him face to face because I believe that there is a human interaction that I cannot predict and no one else can predict' (http://www.theguardian.com/world/2015/apr/27/auschwitz-survivor-angersplaintiffs-trial-forgiveness). Eva Kor claimed that Groning, overwhelmed by her unexpected gesture, fainted. Later she called for prosecutions of SS officers to stop, to allow them to come forward and to explain themselves.

Within these stories of forgiveness and redemption, the Amish community recognized that they were all a part in the story of this tragedy, and Eva Kor understood that forgiveness is an act of self-healing and self-empowerment. The details and facts of the events remain; in fact, these become the vehicle for forgiveness and give the stories their poignancy. Everybody gains through the gift of forgiveness, which transforms fantasies of retribution. We can explore the significance of this further through Japanese protestant theologian Kazo Kitamori (1966), whose *Theology of the Pain of God* is (probably) the first work of Christian theology translated from Japanese). He is writing in the aftermath of the Second World War, genocide, the atomic bombs, and the attitudes of the Japanese and the rest of the world towards each other. Importantly he provides us with an Asian perspective on alterity in relation to transgression, crime and suffering, drawing on both Buddhist traditions and western Christianity (a key difference between Christianity and Buddhism is that the former seeks to embrace and transform suffering whereas the latter seeks to escape it).

Kitamori's (1966) work focuses on the infinite aspects of God's grace (see later) being immanent in an individual's pain. This immanence becomes a revelation. Revelation is the meaning of apocalypse (Gr: *apokaluptein*, literally to uncover), and a key theme of Judaeo-Christianity is the revelation of God's love in times of catastrophe. In times of catastrophe the response is to seek out and support the innocent victim against the guilty perpetrator, but as we have argued (see Chapter 3) in Hebrew the word *avon* denotes harm to both the victim and the perpetrator, with the God of Love and Charity protecting both alike. It is only through the embracing (uncovering) of those who should not be embraced (victim embracing perpetrator, perpetrator embracing victim, community embracing both) that the other is revealed in an economy of grace. Our equality before God and humanity gives us the right to redeem (see Chapter 2) through speech, action and the provision of goods. In so doing, Kitamori returns us to the importance of the body and flesh in the Judaeo-Christian tradition exemplified by a theology of God's immanence in the historical realities of pain for example hungry, thirsty, a stranger, naked, sick, in prison. Punishment makes a victim of the perpetrator and perpetuates the cycle of violence through not providing satisfaction to the original victim, and with the subsequent demand for more punishment. Only love expressed as forgiveness, which enables a reciprocation through repentance, can both recognize the chiasmic structure (see Kitamori, 1966: Chapter 7, n1) and disentangle us from the archaic sacrificial.

Loving and creative practices are the embodiment of flesh, in the form of community that is aware of its own capacity for complicity and is able to mediate between victims and perpetrators (embody the difference), however serious the crime, through working with the natural desires for retribution. The scriptures are relentlessly honest about the difficulty of achieving this but it is our responsibility and not God's. In the words of Merleau-Ponty (cited in Kearney, 2011: 91):

> Christ attests that God would not be fully God without becoming fully man … God is not above but beneath us – meaning that we do not find Him as a suprasensible idea, but as another ourself which dwells in and authenticates our darkness. Transcendence no longer hangs over man; he becomes, strangely, its privileged bearer.

In breaking self-perpetuating cycles of violence, it is incumbent on all the key stakeholders to find a language of giving.

In criminal justice terms there is no longer scope for justice based on exclusion, but a justice based on an embodiment and carrying the burdens (forgiveness and healing) of victims, perpetrators and communities. Girard (1978) argues that the biblical story is a text in travail not only revealing real violence to real people, but also presenting an excess of forgiveness from innocent victims and the consequent development of new identities for 'undeserving' people. In developing these arguments, it is important to use the Girardian distinction between what is sacred and what is holy. The former refers to the sacrificial violent whereby the expulsion or killing of the scapegoat appears to bring about a reductionist solution to the crisis, whereas the latter is concerned with inclusion, wholeness and healing. Reductionist sacrifice (sacred) is at best an interim trade-off in an entropic universe and now that we know that the scapegoat is innocent, we have a major problem with respect to myth and reason, individual and collective action. Luther was correct in seeing individuals not as either good or bad but as both (*simul Justus et peccator*) and our *méconnaissance* coupled with a reductionist mindset means that we have difficulty maintaining this reality. We tend to get alternate views of one or the other, which Žižek (2009: 17) describes as a parallax view:

> The standard definition of a parallax is: the apparent displacement of an object (the shift of its position against a background), caused by a change in observational position that provides a new line of sight. The philosophical twist to be added … is that the observed difference is not simply 'subjective,' due to the fact that the same object which exists 'out there' is seen from two different stances, or points of view.

It is through understanding Jesus' modelling of God's aseity that we can be freed from our own violence, by the invitation to choose a different model as the basis for our relationships, which are distinct from metaphysics (including Nietzschean self-sufficiency), dialectics or teleology (utility or eudaimonism). Community becomes the *ex materia* resource for this new reality, and its development is to be found in an anthropology of gift and theology of grace. As Žižek (2009) argues, epistemological shifts from the subject always reflect an ontological shift in the object itself. For Žižek (2009), the connectedness of being both inside and outside the picture that I perceive bears witness to my material existence, but I cannot see the whole picture as between my perception, and myself is I. Further, this *méconnaissance* (Žižek refers to a blind spot rather than *méconnaissance*) attests to my humanity grounded *ab alio*, and the Judaeo-Christian tradition reveals how to move beyond the scapegoating mechanism in building individual and collective lives.

The repentant thief

In the account of the crucifixion of Jesus, there are fascinating hermeneutical interplays concerning forgiveness, repentance and redemption. According to the Gospel of Luke (read Chapter 23 for the account and quotes later) as Jesus was led away there was a large crowd following, including women who were mourning and lamenting him and who, according to Jewish law, would give sedative drinks to condemned criminals. Jesus says to the women '[i]f this is done to green wood, what will be done when the wood is dry?' (Luke 23: 31). The allusion is to the innocence of Jesus and the false accusations against him; namely if this is how they treat the innocent then how much worse would it be for the guilty? The story builds on this statement, telling that there would be two other 'criminals' executed to the left and right of Jesus (the repentant thief is traditionally known as St Dismas), thus setting up a contrast between innocence and guilt. Meanwhile the ongoing crowd scene (typical of public executions throughout history) is one of a vilification of the condemned. The focus of the text is on Jesus and the challenge from the crowd that if he is the 'chosen one' then why can he not save himself? His response is to say 'Father, forgive them; they do not know what they are doing', and there is an inscription attached to the cross stating '[t]his is the King of the Jews'.

> One of the criminals hanging there abused him: 'Are you not the Christ? Save yourself and save us as well.' But the other spoke up and rebuked him. 'Have you no fear of God at all?' he said. 'You got the same sentence as he did, but in our case we deserved it: we were paying for what we did. But this man has done nothing wrong.' He then said 'Jesus remember me when you come into your kingdom.' He answered him, 'In truth I tell you, today you will be with me in paradise.'

Anthropologically, forgiveness and pardon are functions of Kingship (see the discussion of Derrida in Chapter 3[2]), and despite the statement on the cross being one of mockery and contempt, it unwittingly reveals the truth understood by both of the 'criminals' but not the 'righteous mob'.

This theme of Jesus forgiving his executors and persecutors is historically controversial, with debates about whether the words were in the original scriptures (see Eubank, 2010). For the first two centuries following the time of Jesus, Christianity was essentially a Jewish sect (see Armstrong, 2015), with the similarities leading to violence and the development of historical anti-Semitism (see Schama, 2013 for a detailed discussion). Within this context, the prayer of Jesus on the cross was problematic for early Christians because it seemed to absolve the Jews from killing Jesus. An historical path dependence was instigated, reaching its denouement in the Holocaust and based upon Christianity's own scapegoating and will to power. It explains some of the Protestant Churches' support for Nazi Germany (see Bethge, 2000), and with respect to Catholicism it was not until 2011 that Pope Benedict XVI stated that the Jewish people were not collectively responsible for Jesus' death.

From a hermeneutical perspective the prayer of Jesus on the cross, linked to the story of Dismas, is the key to the Judaeo-Christian tradition and its transformative potential. We accept that within the scriptures there are debates about the limits of forgiveness, but these scriptures indicate that forgiveness within the context of community is the place to begin. The mimetic nature of this approach is clear in the Parable of the Unforgiving Debtor (Matthew, 18: 23–35), where the debtor has his debts cancelled but in turn treats his debtors mercilessly, thus incurring punishment. Either the mimetic cycle can be '[a]n eye for an eye' or treating everybody as our neighbour and returning good for evil in the imitation of God and Jesus (see New Jerusalem Bible, 1984: 1641, fn K).

Saul: from murderer to saint

Saul[3] was complicit in murder and terrorized the early Jesus Movement. Following a conversion event, he went on to become the architect of the Christian Church and arguably western Europe (see Siedentop, 2015). Bartollas' and our research on forgiveness within the criminal justice system (see Pycroft and Bartollas, 2018) has focused on the person of Saul. From a phenomenological perspective, we were interested in his own lived experience of change from being complicit in murder and violence to that of becoming Apostle to the Gentiles. We were intrigued that at no point during or following his conversion did the narratives indicate that he was required to repent or make atonement for his past, and likewise in dealing with the communities that he had previously repressed did he ever deny his past. It would appear that his past was essential to becoming who he was (in some respects, this resonates with Maruna's (2001) work on 'redemption scripts'; in desisting from crime, people became who they always knew that they were). This argument departs from the dialectics of Žižek as there is no 'negation of the negation' that produces a 'new man' (new synthesis); just as the risen Christ is both alive and dead and bears the stigmata of his torture and execution, so Paul is *simul justus et peccator*. He is a radical Jew and his gospel is understood within that context by phenomenologically interpreting *his* religious interpretation to understand what happened to him and his emerging behaviours. However, in interpreting the scriptures we are interpreting the faith community's interpretation of Paul's experience. This developing understanding and emergent theology provides us with the answers that we seek. Žižek (2003) argues that we need to read Paul within the Jewish tradition. He argues that this reveals the true radicalism of Christianity's break with Judaism, but we argue for a continuity of Judaism revealing new resources for working with the relationships between transgression, forgiveness, identity change and rehabilitation in criminal justice for victims, those who break the law, and communities. These relationships are unique (in comparison with other religions) based on Jewish rites that maintain community cohesion rather than promoting exclusion (Douglas, 1999 cited in Barker, 2004). The Pauline story also demonstrates a non-linear understanding of *creatio ex materia*; namely, who he was does not determine who he will become, but who he was is constitutive of who he becomes. This lack of a binary before (Saul) and after conversion (Paul) is clearly demonstrated by the scriptures. Ananias addresses him as Saul (Acts 9: 17), the Holy Spirit refers to him as Saul (Acts 13: 2) and he is referred to as Saul on 11 other occasions following the conversion. Likewise, there is no reference to the 'ex-offender Saul' or 'the violent religious zealot made-good Saul' and this is an important point; his personal history and story are known through his own preaching and writing. His violence and transgression were borne by the community (as the atoning body of Christ) that he had violated (see later).

Saul was born at Tarsus in Cilicia (modern-day Turkey) about 10 CE to a Jewish family. As he says[4] in his own words, '[c]ircumcised on the eighth day, a member of the people of Israel, of the tribe of Benjamin, a Hebrew born of Hebrews, as to the Law a Pharisee' (Philippians 3: 4–9). He was also a (proud) Roman citizen and educated in Jerusalem by Gamaliel, one of the most distinguished teachers of his generation (also making him thoroughly Hellenized) and says 'I advanced in Judaism beyond many of my peers among my race, being especially zealous for the traditions of our ancestors' (Galatians 1: 13–14).

The Pharisees were the most influential of four sects among the Jews (the others being Sadducees, Essenes and Zealots) and believed in resurrection, providence, reward and punishment (Zeitlin, 1941). Paul was a contemporary of Jesus of Nazareth, but other than in the circumstances of his conversion 'event' probably never met him. The point is made by Breton (1988: 34) that when 'Pilate had a title written and put on the cross "Jesus of Nazareth King of the Jews" written in Hebrew, Latin and Greek', then it is tempting to think of Saul's background. Further, Jesus of Nazareth had spent the whole of his short life in the same geographical region, but Paul by his educated background and social/religious status was a cosmopolitan to Jesus' parochialism. With this background and by his temperament he was ideally suited to exporting the gospel message to the wider Roman Empire. The consensus is that Jesus had died circa 30 CE, with Paul's conversion occurring on the road to Damascus circa 34 CE. The vision he had of Jesus during this event changes both his life and the course of world history.

The Acts of the Apostles is very clear about the religious persecution of the Jesus Movement by the religious authorities of the day and the role of Saul. His words 'as to the Law a Pharisee, as to zeal, a persecutor of the church, as to righteousness under the Law, a blameless man' (Philippians 5: 9) tell us interesting things about both his energy and motives in and for his mission, but also that he was justified and had a clear conscience in what he was doing (a key Girardian point, see later). The Temple Guard, following the events surrounding the judicial trial and execution of Jesus of Nazareth, imprisoned various Apostles and a period of unrest seems to have culminated in the stoning to death of Stephen, in which Saul was complicit. Following this religious execution 'a great persecution broke out against the church at Jerusalem ... Saul began to go from house to house, he dragged off men and women and put them in prison' (Acts 8: 1–3).

Saul seems to have been deeply affected by the stoning to death of Stephen, one of the members of the Jesus Movement. The people who were carrying out the stoning laid their cloaks at the feet of Saul, who approved of the stoning (Acts 7: 58). Interestingly the people who laid the cloaks were false witnesses who had lied about Stephen's activities. A religious trial was brought against Jesus and likewise for Stephen. His words as he was being stoned were a mimesis of Jesus' '[f]orgive them Father, for they know not what they do' (Luke 23: 34), in saying 'Lord do not hold this sin against them' (Acts 7: 60). The two events clearly parallel each other and demonstrate an excess of forgiveness from innocent victims. The text refers to the religious clampdown led by Saul following Stephen's stoning: 'Meanwhile Saul was still breathing threats to slaughter the Lord's disciples. He went to the High Priest and asked for letters addressed to the synagogues in Damascus, that would authorise him to arrest and take to Jerusalem any followers of the Way, men or women that he might find' (Acts 9: 1–2). Whatever the exact events, what follows on the road to Damascus changes world history. There are three conversion accounts in Acts 9: 22, Acts 26: 12–18, Galatians 1: 12–17 respectively, but we will focus on Acts 9: 3–19:

> It happened that while he was travelling to Damascus and approaching the city, suddenly a light from heaven shone all around him. He fell to the ground, and then he heard a voice saying, 'Saul, Saul why are you persecuting me?' 'Who are you Lord?' he asked, and the answer came, 'I am Jesus whom you are persecuting. Get up and go into the city, and you will be told what you are to do.' The men travelling with Saul stood there speechless, for though they heard the voice they could see nothing at all, and they had to lead him to Damascus by hand. For three days, he was without his sight and took neither food nor drink.

There was a disciple in Damascus called Ananias and he had a vision in which the Lord said to him, 'Ananias!' When he replied, 'Here I am Lord,' the Lord said 'Get up and go to Straight Street and ask at the house of Judas for someone called Saul, who comes from Tarsus. At this moment he is praying, and has seen a man called Ananias coming in and laying hands on him to give him back his sight.

But, in response, Ananias said, 'Lord, I have heard from many people about this man and all the harm he has been doing to your holy people in Jerusalem. He has come here with a warrant from the chief priests to arrest everybody who invokes your name.' The Lord replied, 'Go for this man is to be my chosen instrument to bring my name before gentiles and kings and before the people of Israel. I myself will show him how much he has to suffer for my name.' Then Ananias went. He entered the house, and laid his hands on Saul and said, 'Brother Saul, I have been sent by the Lord Jesus, who appeared to you on your way here, so that you may recover your sight and be filled with the Holy Spirit.' It was as though scales fell away from his eyes and immediately he was able to see again. So he got up and was baptised, and after taking some food he regained his strength. (New Jerusalem Bible, 1985)

The narrative goes on to describe how only a few days later he began preaching in the synagogues the very gospel he had violently repressed and by proclaiming Jesus as the Christ threw the Jews in Damascus into complete confusion. He went back to Jerusalem with Barnabas, who had taken charge of him (and intriguingly Bar-Nabas translates as both Son of Consolation and Son of Encouragement, thus he is effectively between the victims and the perpetrator). However, the Apostles (church leaders) were all afraid of him, questioned his authenticity and would not accept him. He carried on preaching his 'new gospel' anyway and so the Jews hatched a plot to kill him. He left Jerusalem to go back to Tarsus, and a lull in the panic and chaos ensued. He realized that he was the cause of the problem and left – a voluntary exclusion. The lull in the chaos that followed demonstrated that this realization was correct.

After spending 14 years in Tarsus, he went to Arabia, and became an itinerant tent maker and preacher. During his first missionary journeys (45–49 CE) he started using the Latin name Paul instead of Jewish Saul. He was a person of great dedication and argued a gospel based on Christ crucified and resurrected as universal saviour. In 58 CE he was arrested in Jerusalem, and sent to Rome two years later by Festus the procurator to stand trial, as was his right as a Roman citizen. While in prison, he continued to write epistles to the various churches that he has founded to provide guidance and encouragement. It is unclear what happened to him, though tradition holds that martyrdom followed in Rome in 67 CE.

Interpreting Saul's experience

Saul's dilemma is that the Jesus crucified is alive, having revealed himself to him. His Christophany is an overwhelming experience, which he needs to understand. The way that he would make sense of it (and how we need to interpret his understanding) is through his own background as a Jew and Pharisee. We are told that immediately after the event he was in prayer and he was fasting (purifying himself) in keeping with religious observance. He knows that anyone who dies on a tree is cursed (Deuteronomy 21: 23) and yet this Jesus is clearly blessed by God and has consequently been resurrected from the dead despite being crucified. This immediately calls into question the link between ritual purity and sin, part of the rationale for his repression of the new Christians. Then, a representative of the very community that he has been persecuting comes to him with an act of superabundant grace, naming him as brother and embracing him. This would reinforce what Paul had witnessed at the execution of Stephen, namely a forgiving victim. This unconditional forgiveness allows Saul to see that he had been complicit in violence, and wrong in his actions, despite being justified by the law and therefore his conscience.

He was then baptised. Although little is known about the Apostle Paul's own baptism, his theological writings about baptism are marked by belief in the superabundant grace of God that overwhelms the human deficit of sin. Offered without regard to birth, ancestry, social status or behaviour (Romans 9: 6–18), baptism was the Church's witness to the indiscriminate, unconditional, unconditioned, uncontingent, unmerited and unstinting gifting of God for the beginning of a new life. Perhaps conceived by Paul as like the clothing of young people at coming-of-age ceremonies (Harill, 2002), baptism marked an undeserved new start. No one was deserving of the grace of God. Everything in this new life, even faith itself, is attributed to God's 'gratia gratuita' (Prof Esther Reed, private correspondence). A declaration of fundamental identity in Christ removes all distinctions and is the basis for a radical equality before God and man and where in the rite of baptism (particularly child baptism) the community makes promises on behalf of the child. In all of these examples of baptism there is no repentance as baptism removes all sin. To put this another way, acceptance into the community removes sin, contra the removal of sin being a prerequisite for acceptance into the community.

The answer then to the question of why Paul was not required to atone, repent or make good for his wrongdoing to the Christian community would have been understood in the community of his time. In the emerging practices of the Eucharistic meal, understood within the context of Judaism, the community did not focus on his crimes but on creating a new and communal space of potentiality. This is the truth of forgiveness (see Pycroft and Bartollas, 2018); redemption is a beginning rather than an end state and is the true monstrosity of Christ (see Davis, 2009) and his demonstration to the world of being wrong about sin and judgement based on exclusion and death (John 16: 8–9).

Incarnational grace

The Jewish focus on place, laying bare, and the unveiling of *méconnaissance* is the Pauline story of grace and both its superabundant distinctiveness from the equivalence of the *lex talionis* (see Millie, 2016) and incongruity relative to worth. This outpouring of grace is the model for responding to crime and transgression, not the abdication to a metaphysical god, but taking responsibility and acting as if God did not exist (see Chapter 7 and the discussion of Bonhoeffer's New Theology). The work of Derrida and the concept of the perfect gift is discussed at length by Barclay (2015), with Derrida arguing that the perfect gift is one that is free of any reciprocity. Barclay argues that this concept is a modern one, in part stemming from Luther's view that God gives freely, and reaches a universal ethical ideal in Kantian philosophy whereby we freely choose personal constraints based on reason alone. This approach contrasts with archaic societies where social solidarity, status and honour are configured within the economy of the gift (see, for example, Mauss, 1997). Within a process of redemption there needs to be a genuine and reciprocal encounter that enables repentance. This may well involve aspects of grace as a gift with respect to the spirit in which it is given, its timing, appropriateness, efficacy and whether it is reciprocated, but nonetheless it stems from forgiveness.

Paul preaches a gospel of grace based upon his own experience of forgiveness, received from the communities that he has oppressed. He and the communities involved understand that grace is a gift to undeserving people, and that repentance is an engagement with that gift. Luther's theology is fundamentally concerned with overcoming and removing the anxiety in humanity's relationship to God (Hanson and Hanson, 1985). In this theology and the practices of religion, the last vestiges of religious sacrifice disappear with the revelation not of God's forgiveness of humankind but rather that we can forgive each other. This perspective develops out of the ancient Jewish rite of *kpr*, which translates as atonement and which protected against divine wrath and destruction. These were indicative of the breakdown of the divine order through a covenant of peace, which maintained creation by ordering and binding the forces of chaos. With the re-establishing of the covenant through atonement creation was renewed. Barker quotes from Mary Douglas (1999) that

> according to illustrative cases from Leviticus, to atone means to recover, cover again, to repair a hole, cure a sickness, mend a rift, make good a torn or broken covering ... atonement does not mean covering a sin so as to hide it from the sight of God; it means making good an outer layer which has been rotted or pierced. (Douglas, 1999, cited in Barker, 2004: 45)

As Marshall (2021) argues, atonement in this sense is less about remitting guilt, and more concerned with stemming the contagion (mimetic action) of sin. *Kpr* is effected in the Temple, which was the meeting place of heaven and earth, with the holy of holies being simultaneously heaven and earth. Rituals of atonement were also creation and covenant rituals. The role of the High Priest was significant; he wore a gold plate on his forehead showing the name *yhwh*, a name that only the purified could speak. Further, Barker argues that the evidence suggests the High Priest in this context functions as the LORD, who, as the author of creation, is making atonement to prevent his own wrath bringing about disastrous consequences. For Barker the incarnation of Jesus as the son of God is understood in this sense but historically has been interpreted differently, with the idea of atonement as giving satisfaction to an angry and demanding God (see Chapter 3). In the symbolism of temple atonement, blood is life and when the actions of *kpr* were performed, the object was not a person but a place or a thing – that is, places were sprinkled with blood to cleanse, consecrate from the un-cleanliness of the people. Barker (2004: 46) quotes from the *Jewish Encyclopeadia*: 'In the prophetic language, however, the original idea of the atonement offering had become lost, and instead of the offended person (God) *the offence or guilt became the object of atonement*' (emphasis in the original).

Barker argues that the role of the priests, the LORD and the scapegoat (see Chapter 4) is to 'carry' the iniquity of the people. *Kpr*, when translated as bear, carry or forgive, means that the iniquity was carried (absorbed) through eating the flesh of the sin offering whose blood had been used for *kpr* and through the High Priest functioning as the LORD. The latter indicates that the role of the priest/LORD was to hold his people together rather than separating the ritually impure. By extension when Jesus says, '[i]f you do not eat the flesh of the Son of Man and drink his blood, you have no life in you' (John 6: 53) he is fulfilling the same function, but the Greek translation for flesh that is used is *sarx*. *Sarx* refers to all that is carnal and lustful, and literally refers to animal nature and the meat of an animal. Therefore, at the last supper and the institution of the Eucharistic meal (Luke 22: 14–20) the invitation is to participate in absorbing, bearing and carrying the transgressions (mimetic desires) of the community through eating the body and blood (*sarx*) of Christ (in the form of bread and wine). The Council of Trent of the Roman Catholic Church reminds us of the human condition and that human nature (not God) demands sacrifice (Chapman, 2014). Therefore, the Eucharist as a God-given bloodless sacrifice is a remembrance of both innocent victims and our violence and complicity in violence to the scapegoats of history (anthropological initial conditions). This anamnesis opens new spaces of possibility to appropriate new forms of energy and to make real the possibilities that flow from forgiveness and rejecting sacrifice. This outflowing of grace to the community actualizes redemption as a gift to the other.

Repentance

Despite having such a prominent place in the Judeo-Christian tradition, the Hebrew language has no specific word for repentance (Moore, 1927). The word *teshubah* denotes to go back, to turn about and ultimately to return to God. In the New Testament, the Greek translation is *metanoia*, with a literal meaning of beyond or after thought. However, significantly in Greek mythology Metanoia is a Goddess who is the consort of Kairos, the God of Opportunity. Therefore, whereas Metanoia's concern was for the missed moment, shrouded in sorrow and shadow, Kairos presents a new and immanent time for action. Our reading of repentance is the gift to the other emerging from a radical alterity between the perpetrator and the victim, who have experienced a mutual non-being in a moment in time. Repentance is the necessary corollary to forgiveness in acknowledging both guilt and the potential for being, with an invitation to the other to speak truth. Neither forgiveness nor repentance changes the ontology of the event, however the generative potential of grace both projects and actualizes a new reality. Forgiveness and repentance overcome the dissipative structure of satisfaction as no trade-off is required in the form of a sacrifice of the other, nor is the self reduced or diminished. Dismas acknowledges that truth and Jesus' immanent affirmation again cause historic consternation to a developing institutional Church (for example how is his salvation possible without having to jump through the sacerdotal hoops of baptism and so on?).

In the meeting of the phenomenology of both the victim and the criminal, all of the dynamics of past, present and future are present. Some aspects are virtual (for example the future and some aspects of the past, although the consequences of trauma may be actualized somatically and psychologically, with fear and anxiety forward looking) and some actualized. Forgiveness first enables an immanent repentance and thus an actualization of the new, which is a revelation of who both victim and criminal are in themselves.

Wounds and scars

The impacts of crime are real, as are the impacts of punishment, with both leaving wounds and scars. A return to an understanding of flesh and what is actual helps us to embrace the wounded other and at least a suturing of the dehiscence between and within ourselves. This is necessary in building both universal and preferential solidarity, with the scars themselves (those which are seen and those which are unseen) acting as memorials. As Ashley (2015) explains, Metz's theology counters the idea of the entropic universe and the myth of endless time stretching out behind and before us (see Chapter 2) as this renders both remembrance and radical transformation ridiculous. He argues for an apocalyptic temporality bounded not by an ever-receding horizon (itself bounded by nothingness) but by a loving, just God who meets us and changes the course of things. Importantly Metz's approach is an existential stance within history that both complains to God concerning injustices experienced and praises Him for good things. Ontologically this reality is a part of the structure of *simul justus et peccator* and our own understanding and laying bare of complicity and new possibilities.

Rambo (2015) argues that wounds are central to the Christian story and that it is through these wounds that truth in the form of theories of redemption, salvation and sacred stories of creation and recreation pour. She considers wounds within the context of trauma (the word translated from the Greek for wound) and the ways in which wounds may be both seen and unseen. Rambo (2015) conceives of a wound as a death involving a multi-sensory shattering of meaning, and thus any afterlife (we would say recovery, or more appropriately discovery – see Pycroft, 2021b) involves a multi-sensory reconstitution of life and having the features of a scar. This working through wounds requires a theorization of matter, sight and sound given the somatic features of trauma.

A function of liturgy is an anamnesis of the crucifixion of the innocent Jesus, and in the Catholic and Orthodox traditions makes this one sacrifice available in all time to all people. Yet Jesus still has his wounds after the resurrection (see particularly the Gospel of John) and for Rambo (2015) this raises an important question of whether the wounds of trauma are opened continually, even after death, or whether complete healing is possible. In this respect, scars are important because they represent healing with memory. Memories are deep, personal, timeless and unrepresentable whereas scars can be touched and read and form boundaries between the individual and society, and in our argument between victim and perpetrator. In this sense, the scar can be a social site of witness and creative healing (Rambo, 2015) a site of incarnate meaning (Rosenberg, 2018).

6

Actualization

An act of punishment or its effects will not lead to a good life (Gr: *eudaimon*). Punishment as a metaphysical and rationally calculated moral equivalence to a harm done perpetuates violence. If this approach were effective in changing behaviours then the harshness of current penal systems would see the courts, prisons and probation caseloads radically reduced. The actuarial in criminal justice treats the virtual as real and through closing down the phase space of encounter (taking away rather than giving energy) ensures the locking in of failure. The teleological enterprise of rehabilitation, with its emphasis on risk and public protection, cannot actualize what is truly human; thus, the creation of a self-perpetuating pathology becomes its own frame of reference, devoid of achievement or human value (see Bettelheim, 1960). Rather than perpetuating violence, redemption is the actualization of possibility (the infinite in the finite), changes made real rather than remaining virtual and achieved by holding open what can be variously described as the 'gate of repentance' (Moore, 1927: 529), the initiatory dimension (Oughourlian, 2012) or the inauguration of an eschatology, where we meet and accept the person as they are within an immanent space. This space is one of love, where the gaze of truth enables an enfleshment of that which has hitherto only been imagined (virtual).

Idols and icons

Stanislas Breton (1988: 105) states:

> Although it does not pose an unsolvable problem, the Greek *Eikon* can be translated in two different ways ... *image* (as the theologians have decided) evokes the idea of a reproductive likeness ... More discreet, less determinate, *icon,* accentuates the traces of a face and the contours of a figure. 'Emanation of the glory of the Almighty, spotless mirror and reflection,' it hearkens back to the description of Wisdom in the book of that same name. We do not have to choose. Or, if we choose both, it is because the 'invisible God' (probably an allusion to the 'hidden God' of Isaiah 45.15, *who became the* deus absonditus *of the tradition and perhaps inspired the* homo absconditus *of Ernst Bloch*[1]*) does not tolerate or favor one translation over another.* Taken as distinct from

the *Unknown God* of the negative theologies, this invisible and hidden God is revealed as much in the undulation of a light as in the light of a face. (emphasis added)

An idol is produced by the gaze that looks at it whereas an icon provokes a new vision, rather than being a result of that vision (Marion, 2012). An icon interrupts rather than confirms existing perspectives. In the highly deterministic structures in which we exist and live, we only catch glimpses of these possibilities through the undulating light, but usually a personal crisis engenders the need for a new vision, a new model for our desire. These crises free us from acquisitive mimesis, and the projection of our non-being. Revealed as ontologically both light and shade, the invitation for every human being is to overcome themself and their desire for violence, a victory over the self rather than a victory over others. This non-bloody combat (exemplified in the Eucharist) produces winners without victims and without the need for purification through the production of scapegoats (Oughourlian, 2012).

To borrow from the theological thought of Japanese artist Makoto Fujimura (2020) we can produce a criminology of making where we become culture makers, creators of new realities not grounded in violence. This project of alterity does not dismiss or sublimate the suffering of the innocent victim but rather offers a new culture actualizing a multiplicity in unity (see Chapter 2) where there is no hierarchy of gifts or scale of imperfection. In her biography of Girard, Cynthia Haven (2018) cites the Dante scholar John Freccero as saying that what terrifies us is the thought that all people are born equal. This equality (and thus, fear) stems from the individuality that separates each person from the other, that each is individual, equal and diverse but united in one creation (Lane and Price, 2005). This endowment of each person with absolute, universal, inalienable and inviolable rights means that they are already whole: equality is the acknowledgement, embrace and positive response to the whole humanity of the other. This ontological structuring has declined in modernity through reductive method and the objectification of time and Newtonian physics (see Chapter 2), 'whose events are related diachronically purely by efficient causal relations, and synchronically by mutual conditioning' (Taylor, 1989: 288). How we relate our lives to this time matters, with Taylor (1989) arguing the importance of storytelling and life narration where the story is drawn from events and circumstances. He says that in the objectified world meanings are consequential to events, making autobiography more difficult as narrated meanings unfold *through* the events to create identity (subjectivity) in the self-narration. The Judaeo-Christian perspective is that personal (subjective) or social crisis interrupts this 'world-time' (the link between chronology and causality) to reveal a new narrative (poiesis) grounded in the eschaton (a catastrophe becomes an apocalypse) and a gathering of all time into eschatological time.

Eschatological time reveals that a freely given gift of grace generates new possibilities and at least the beginning of a new image (*icon*) for both victim and criminal. In theological terms, just as God has chosen us first, then we choose to choose the other first. This is clearly expressed by William Wilberforce, who was sitting in his garden looking bewildered when his butler asked him what was wrong, and he responded by saying that it was God. The butler questioned whether he had found God, and Wilberforce responded that God had found him. It is through seeing people as they are and embracing them *simul justus et pecator* that the virtual can be actualized; in the case of Wilberforce he led the movement to ban slavery in the UK. Wilberforce held open the gates of repentance, which ultimately led to global changes in our understanding of what it means to be human. There are numerous other examples of iconic activists, many of whom will never be known beyond their local communities.

Sam Dillon

Growing up on the streets of Chicago, Sam joined the Blackstone Raiders and became one of the 'Main 21', the main leaders of this gang. He was appointed as the Enforcer of the gang, which meant he was responsible for punishing those committing gang violations. He describes this role: 'If someone violated or stepped out of line, they had to deal with us. I was responsible for controlling the North Side and parts of Woodlawn. I have been shot and stabbed on different occasions, and this made me very ruthless. Life became very cheap for me' (Bartollas et al, 2019: 248).

Sam eventually received a 14–20-year sentence for homicide and was released after nine years and three months, but he continued his involvement with the gang and was charged with a double homicide. He was on the run for eight years and featured on the television show, *America's Most Wanted Criminals*; Sam did not feel guilty about those he had harmed as he regarded it as his work for the gang. He completed nine years of his sentence, leaving prison a changed person following a conversion experience: 'I had a religious experience and came to know that God was indeed real. I also realized that the list of people who had to be dealt with was too long' (Bartollas, 2019). He started to engage with the implications of this experience and in prison he began and finished his college diploma and decided to get his Master's degree and work with young gang members in the community and penal institutions. Because there was a hit on him, Sam's friends sent him out of state to do his graduate degree in sociology, where he gained a number of friends in and out of the graduate programme who supported him. Sam relapsed a number of times with his drinking behaviours at which times he was not pleasant to be around. Following the completion of his graduate work, he has worked with gang youth in Iowa and Minnesota's institutions. He developed serious physical problems and died in 2019 but from the time of his last release from prison, 15 years before, he no longer associated with the gang or became involved in any form of illegal behaviour.

Kathy Boudin

On 7 September 2003 Kathy Boudin was released from the Bedford Hills correctional facility, ending a 22-year sentence at the prison which left a mark on both prisoners and the institution. On 20 October 1981 Boudin, a member of the militant organization 'Weather Underground', had served as a decoy in the passenger seat of a U-Haul van in Nanuet, New York. Following the robbery of a Brink's armoured truck, and the killing of three men and serious injury of another, she pleaded guilty to first-degree robbery and second-degree murder, receiving a sentence of 20 years to life. Boudin did not deny what she had done but wanted something constructive to come from her life, and in the years following her incarceration she reshaped that life. Boudin went to work at the prison children's centre in 1984, becoming an inmate coordinator for the parenting classes and the teen programme. In 1994 college courses in prison were discontinued throughout the US, and Kathy Boudin approached Michelle Fine, Professor of Psychology at the Graduate Center of City University, New York, and they worked together to re-establish college courses at the prison. Eventually, they were able to get 12 colleges and universities to contribute faculty resources pro bono within the prison and it worked very well. In her 22 years at the Bedford Hills correctional facility she developed more than a dozen programmes and was paroled in 2003.

Following her release, Boudin accepted a job as an AIDS counsellor at St Luke's Roosevelt Hospital Center in New York City and received a doctorate from Columbia University, Teachers College. She is co-Director and co-founder of the Center for Justice at Columbia University (https://socialwork.columbia.edu/faculty-research/faculty/research-scientists/kathy-boudin/). She says that it was not always easy facing her long sentence, and in spite of what she was doing for prisoners and the development of programmes for them, the parole board twice turned her down. Her son Chesa, who was 14 months old when his mother were convicted, has become the District Attorney for San Francisco, and in opposition to his election the local Deputy Sherriff's Union referred to him as 'son of terrorists' and '#1 choice of criminals and gang members' (https://www.theguardian.com/us-news/2019/nov/16/son-of-jailed-radicals-reviled-by-the-police-union-now-chesa-boudin-is-san-franciscos-top-cop). This despite a law degree from Yale University and two Master's degrees from Oxford

University, where he was a Rhodes Scholar. This is a classic example of the conferring of punishment on the children of the guilty to try and counter what are seen as overly lenient approaches to punishment which challenge the penal–industrial complex.

Minister Rico Johnson, godfather of the Vice Lord Nation

Rico went to prison and after nearly 20 years he was paroled in 1980. He continued to commit crimes. At times, he hurt others. He was convinced that he had to deal harshly with certain people and that failing to do so would show weakness and put his status as a leader in jeopardy among his peers. Following his imprisonment at Stateville Correctional Center, Rico believed that adopting Islam would supply what was missing in his life. With an able mentor, Joseph Ussef, he became committed to the philosophy, practices and expected behaviours of the Muslim faith. His own conversion to Islam led him to spearhead the conversion of the Conservative Vice Lords, both those who were imprisoned and those in the community, and he himself became a minister of the faith. Yet despite his religious conversion, when Rico was released from prison in 1980, he returned to the streets. Forsaking his new-found beliefs, he committed whatever crimes he had to in order to become king of the hill. He particularly wanted control of the drug trade in Chicago. In a little over two years, his luck ran out, both with the Chicago Police Department and other gangs, and he was apprehended and returned to the Illinois Department of Corrections with a long sentence. Significantly, after he returned to prison he reaffirmed his commitment to Allah and Muslim practices. He had to learn a more mature expression of the Islamic faith and beliefs, a gradual process that has taken place since the early 1980s. Was his redemption true and lasting? The passage of time indicates it has been. Another aspect of Rico's redemptive script is the positive effect that he had on other inmates as a minister during his incarceration. When a number of the inmates he worked with were released, they turned away from drugs and crime and have since attempted to improve their communities – some of them for 20 or 30 years. Over a decade or more, numerous individuals whom Rico counselled have maintained a crime-free and drug-free lifestyle. Rico has continued to express and promote this redemptive philosophy since his release from prison in August 2012. As he put it, his goal is 'to save the children'. He believes his life's mission is to make a difference in the lives of the young so that they will not continue their involvement in crime and drugs and waste years in prison as he did. Other leaders in the community who began as gang members have turned their lives around as well. Rico has found various ways to be a positive force in others' lives. To cite one instance, he feeds over 150 families a day (Bartollas, 2019: xi and xii).

These stories of redemption of course are not the norm for criminal justice. For the majority of people engaged with prison, probation and rehabilitation services more generally, there is no life change as they are caught in the revolving door of the sacred sacrificial. Nonetheless, these redemption scripts reveal a number of interesting dynamics:

The necessary sin of Adam

Despite doctrinal controversies, there is a genuine Judaeo–Christian tradition of the coexistence of sin and grace in the soul (see Tugwell, 1979; the following discussion is indebted to Tugwell's exegesis), meaning that every criminal act opens the possibility of a redemptive act. Grace is discovered in an event and not from a general sense of the benevolence of God (Barclay, 2015). For Macarius of Egypt (4th Century CE) (see Mason, 2020) the gift of grace does not remove sin once and for all, or mean that we should increasingly be punished harshly when we inevitably relapse after we are gifted something. Rather, what is real about sin and transgression is not its definition in law (legal or theological) but its actuality as a part of life. If God created repentance before the creation of the world (see Chapter 3) then that is because sin and transgression is inevitable, and we can only come to understand our reliance on God through that sin. In the view of St Irenaeus (*c.* 130–202 CE), Adam was not created perfect, and sin which has no being in and of itself (it is always relative, *ab alio*) does not change the part of us that is always united with God (*esse qua esse bonum est*). This is expressed in the Easter proclamation sung by Christians to mark the resurrection of Jesus containing the words *O felix culpa* (Latin: O happy fault):

> O truly necessary sin of Adam,
> Destroyed completely by the Death of Christ!
> O happy fault, that earned for us so great, so glorious a Redeemer!

The Hebrew *avon* (see Chapter 3), meaning both crime and punishment, is indicative that the transgression is the source of redemption through forgiveness. It is not our task to add to this suffering but to embrace that person as a whole, including the transgression. These themes are explored in the work of the writer Shūsaku Endō (see Hoekema, 2000; Kasza, 2016) providing us (along with Kitamori – see Chapter 5) a Christian (in this case Catholic) perspective influenced by Japanese Buddhism. In his novels and plays, he demonstrates that good things can lie hidden in what is evil and that no human is purely evil, and the necessary sin of Adam is how we come to know God and receive redemption. As with Kitamori, Endō has no use for Christ, Pantocrator, the judgemental and triumphant king of the world: 'Love goes beyond judgement ... even if that seems useless from a rational point of view' (Hoekema, 2000: 245). Likewise, Henryk Górecki, in conversation about his Symphony of Sorrowful Songs (Palmer, 2007), says of music concerned with death, separation and the Holocaust that '[w]e need to see the good in every person, no matter how evil'. But in apprehending that good we have to respond.

Forgiveness as anterior gift

The gift of forgiveness (see Chapter 3) does not require remorse but it does enable a virtual appreciation by the criminal that the relationship with the victim and wider society can be different. Likewise, the victim can perceive the possibility of a different relationship with the criminal. A key difference between Hellenist thinking and that of the Hebrew Bible is that the first is concerned with ahistorical and metaphysical categories whereas the latter is historicist in the sense of seeking to place events in time and space. In the theology of Johann Baptist Metz (see Ashley, 2015) the rationality of the Hebrew Bible is one of anamnesis and remembrance, linked to narrative and solidarity. The memory in question is that of the authenticity of the innocent victim and ensuring that they and their story do not disappear from history. There can be no passive phenomenology towards the past but rather an engagement in dangerous stories told and retold in the name of freedom for both individuals and society. For Christians the paradigmatic memory is the death and resurrection of Jesus Christ, recalled in the Eucharistic feast, and which continually opens us up to other crucified people in our past and present.

Repentance

Repentance (see Chapter 5) is the choice to attempt to reciprocate the gift of forgiveness and requires actions on the part of the criminal in responding and engaging with the possibilities that have emerged from their crimes. This enables the victim to perceive an actualization of being over non-being. In Metz's theology,

> narrative involves the one who hears with the experiences narrated. It is a sacramental reality, one which produces a community with the other who is telling the story, and with the subjects of the narrative itself. It is a community within a history which is still ongoing, which cannot be encompassed theoretically. (Ashley, 2015: 162)

In the process of speaking my truth, nothing is covered, nothing forgotten and both the narrator and the listener, embodied in the narrative, are changed and enabled to bring those crucified down from the cross.

Storytelling

Storytelling leads to hope, solidarity and the opening up rather than closing down of possibility. Encouragement from others is essential in embracing a new identity that holds both the crime and the new identity in superposition, namely they are co-constitutive of each other. As Metz argues, this does not take away our complaint to God about the injustice we have suffered but in solidarity with others we can actualize hope (influenced by Ernst Bloch – discussed in Chapter 2). There is an almost universal consensus that the maintenance of any personal change is non-linear and that relapse is the norm rather than the exception. This is because the individual contains the potential of both being and non-being. However, in the processes of retributive justice this is inverted so that what is normal is treated as abnormal and addressed even more harshly (see Pycroft, 2021b). Depending upon the type of behaviour and crime, relapse is a high-risk proposition for the community. However, social solidarity is created through the remembrance of victims, being open to the suffering of the present, and through imitating Christ .embracing those who should not be embraced.

Actualization and maturation grow as commitment and steadfastness to being over non-being. Metz argues that universal and preferential solidarity complement one another as the first can become totalizing and the second hateful demonization. He argues that it is through commitment and engagement that the lives of subjects are nourished and actualized in action on behalf of others. The story to be told is a redemption script (Maruna, 2001), whether relating to low level or serious crime, as in the economy of grace there is no scale of imperfection; whatever the crime, the person is embraced. A new truth event or series of truth events emerge from that embrace in the *ex materia* exchange of energy (see Chapter 2), rather than *ex nihilo* that is, it is not possible to pull ourselves up by our own bootstraps. History is replete with examples of people who, like St Paul (Chapter 5), have committed crimes or transgressions but gone on to have a significant impact for good, seen as icons, but in practice are the exceptions that prove the reality of modern rehabilitation. The double transference of condemnation and exaltation reinforce the need for scapegoats. A contemporary example of these dynamics is in the theology, philosophy and practices of Alcoholics Anonymous (AA) (and other 12-step programmes).

Alcoholics Anonymous

AA is possibly the major contribution of Protestant evangelical theology to modernity. It is an example of where redemption as the embodiment of difference, through grace (expressed as a Higher Power) inverts the structures normally associated with punishment and rehabilitation. This embodiment as a feedback loop creates its own possibility, the anterior gift of membership of a community of scapegoats meeting people where they are and as they are in themselves. An iconic organization, it provokes a new theological rather than clinical vision[2] for people by embracing those who should not be embraced. Being generatively 'bottom up' and self-organizing (see Figure 6.1), there is a contrast with a range of statutory and non-statutory institutions and organizations that have to compete to exist in the neoliberal market place. To use Paul Ricoeur's (2004) argument, such utilitarian institutions have no moral conscience, and consequently, when confronted with the guilt of others, we simply rehash old grievances and ancient humiliations and despite best intentions cannot escape using others for our own utilitarian interests as we constantly calculate the benefits that our actions will bring for ourselves. This is a good example of the inability of organizations such as the UK Metropolitan Police to address the problem of institutional racism, that is, if racism is institutional how do we address the issue at the individual level of the police officer (see Grieve, 2014) to deal with their own individual *méconnaissance*? The organization of AA through the 12 traditions (see Figure 6.2) demonstrates why it has been as successful as it avoids an entanglement with other organizations and thus other people's priorities. In AA, individuals are invited to choose a different model for their desire and in that sense, it is not about alcohol, which is named only in the first step:

> In simplest form, the AA program operates when a recovered alcoholic passes along the story of his or her own problem drinking, describes the sobriety he or she has found in AA, and invites the newcomer to join the informal Fellowship. The heart of the suggested programme of personal recovery is contained in Twelve Steps (see [Figure 6.1]) describing the experience of the earliest members of the Society. Newcomers are not asked to accept or follow these Twelve Steps in their entirety if they feel unwilling or unable to do so. They will usually be asked to keep an open mind, to attend meetings at which recovered alcoholics describe their personal experiences in achieving sobriety, and to read AA literature describing and interpreting the AA program. AA members will usually emphasize to newcomers that only problem drinkers themselves, individually, can determine whether or not they are in fact alcoholics. At the same time, it will be pointed out that all available medical testimony indicates that alcoholism is a progressive illness, that it cannot be cured in the ordinary sense of the term, but that it can be arrested through total abstinence from alcohol in any form. (https://www.alcoholics-anonymous.org.uk/about-aa/the-12-steps-of-aa)

Figure 6.1: Twelve steps of Alcoholics Anonymous

---

1. We admitted we were powerless over alcohol – that our lives had become unmanageable.

2. Came to believe that a Power greater than ourselves could restore us to sanity.

3. Made a decision to turn our will and our lives over to the care of God as we understood Him.

4. Made a searching and fearless moral inventory of ourselves.

5. Admitted to God, to ourselves and to another human being the exact nature of our wrongs.

6. Were entirely ready to have God remove all these defects of character.

7. Humbly asked Him to remove our shortcomings.

8. Made a list of all persons we had harmed, and became willing to make amends to them all.

9. Made direct amends to such people wherever possible, except when to do so would injure them or others.

10. Continued to take personal inventory and when we were wrong promptly admitted it.

11. Sought through prayer and meditation to improve our conscious contact with God as we understood Him, praying only for knowledge of His will for us and the power to carry that out.

12. Having had a spiritual awakening as the result of these steps, we tried to carry this message to alcoholics and to practice these principles in all our affairs.

Source: https://www.alcoholics-anonymous.org.uk/about-aa/the-12-steps-of-aa

Communities of scapegoats

The steps from 1 to 12 are reiterative and an example of a positive feedback loop that generates new possibilities. Lillian Dykes (2001) states that AA provides us with a laboratory wherein the theories of Girard have been applied, but also this experiment in living non-violently reveals the double transference of condemnation and exaltation. Namely, we condemn those who are 'out of control' due to 'their' desire for alcohol (and we can add every compulsion, for example sex, drugs, sport – there are now a plethora of 12-step programmes for different behaviours) and yet both insist on and applaud the very abstinence that we reject for ourselves. Further, my compulsions expressed as constitutional rights to alcohol, particular foodstuffs, guns and so on creates communities of scapegoats, which reassures me that my behaviour is 'normal' and not compulsive. Across human behaviours Pareto's Law seems to apply, with its 20/80 split, for example 20 per cent of people consume 80 per cent of alcohol or 20 per cent of offenders commit 80 per cent of crimes, and so policymakers have focused on the 20 per cent. The problem with this approach is that by focusing on the 20 per cent and removing them from the equation, deterministic factors related to supply and availability mean that others (see Holder, 1999 and Pycroft, 2014) replace these people. As

Figure 6.2: Twelve traditions of Alcoholics Anonymous

---

1. Our common welfare should come first; personal recovery depends upon AA unity.

2. For our group purpose there is but one ultimate authority – a loving God as He may express Himself in our group conscience. Our leaders are but trusted servants; they do not govern.

3. The only requirement for AA membership is a desire to stop drinking.

4. Each group should be autonomous except in matters affecting other groups or AA as a whole.

5. Each group has but one primary purpose – to carry its message to the alcoholic who still suffers.

6. An AA group ought never endorse, finance or lend the AA name to any related facility or outside enterprise, lest problems of money, property and prestige divert us from our primary purpose.

7. Every AA group ought to be fully self-supporting, declining outside contributions.

8. Alcoholics Anonymous should remain forever nonprofessional, but our service centers may employ special workers.

9. AA, as such, ought never be organized; but we may create service boards or committees directly responsible to those they serve

10. Alcoholics Anonymous has no opinion on outside issues; hence the AA name ought never be drawn into public controversy.

11. Our public relations policy is based on attraction rather than promotion; we need always maintain personal anonymity at the level of press, radio and films.

12. Anonymity is the spiritual foundation of all our traditions, ever reminding us to place principles before personalities.

While the Twelve Traditions are not specifically binding on any group or groups, an overwhelming majority of members have adopted them as the basis for AA's expanding internal and public relationships.

Source: https://www.alcoholics-anonymous.org.uk/about-aa/aa-traditions

an example, there is incontrovertible evidence for the relationships between population-level consumption of alcohol and a range of harms (including dependence) in that population (Edwards et al, 1995): the higher the level of consumption the higher the levels of a range of harms. The clear message is that to reduce those harms we should all consume less alcohol and reduce supply and availability to help others, even if we do not have a 'problem', but for most people this is unacceptable and an infringement of the right of our desire. That desire is of supreme economic value to the perpetuation of the acquisitive mimesis of others (for example, think of the role of the alcohol, tobacco, food and gun industries in preventing population-level behavioural change). That is why we condemn and ultimately murder our prophets and the historical role models who live and promote non-violence. These include, for example, Jesus, Paul, Gandhi and Martin Luther King but also those who call for gun law reform in the US, or reform of drug, alcohol and mental health policy. In the case of Jesus, he signed his own death warrant because his religious teachings were anthropological, challenging the economic basis of the temple, revealing the truth of 'the economy of the sacred' (Keddie, 2019: 153) and its exclusionary practices. The corrections-industrial complex is the economy of the sacred (Pycroft, 2021b), with any challenge to that system striking our compulsive desires for sacrifice and thus the very foundations of contemporary economic social order.

The economy of the sacred

The hermeneutical key is the account of Jesus cleansing the Temple. The accounts from Matthew's Gospel and that of John are very similar (Matthew has the events following Jesus' triumphal entry into Jerusalem and building up to his trial and execution, whereas John places them at the beginning of Jesus' ministry. Either way the consequences will be catastrophic for Jesus):

> The Passover of the Jews was near, and Jesus went up to Jerusalem. In the Temple, he found people selling cattle, sheep and doves, and the moneychangers seated at their tables. Making a whip of cords, he drove them all out of the Temple, both sheep and the cattle. He also poured out the coins of the moneychangers and over turned their tables. He told those who were selling the doves 'Take these things out of here! Stop making my Father's house a marketplace!' (John 2: 13–17)

Simon Schama's work (2013) vividly describes the permanent pall of wood smoke over the city, the smells of charring flesh from the ritual cremation (holocaust) of whole animals. This required the bringing of thousands of animals into the city from surrounding areas to supply this conveyor belt of sacrifice, morning and afternoon as required by the Torah (and additional sacrifices on holy days). The most prized animal skins went to the High Priest, who might then bestow them on other priests, and to feed the multitude of pilgrims there would be 'pop-up' vendors around the city. This attack was deliberate and real. The moneychangers were there to convert the international currencies of the pilgrims coming to the temple, enabling payment for an animal sacrifice. Keddie describes the institutional power of the economy of the sacred and the interdependence of religious and economic activities (2019: 152–3) thus:

> [T]he priestly elites who controlled the Jerusalem Temple were instrumental in the economic and cultural integration of Palestine into the Roman Empire as well as the continuation of the Judaeans' indigenous religious traditions. As agents of God and brokers of the

sacred, Jerusalem's priestly elites were self-interested in maintaining traditional Judaean worship but also in increasing their own wealth and power. Through their progressively political positions within one of Jerusalem's foremost economic institutions (the Temple cult), Judaean priestly elites played a part in specifying property rights, and attaining profits from other worshippers' transaction costs. They often derived divine support for their positions within Judaean society through particular interpretations of the Torah – that is, by harnessing ideological power.

Runions (2021: 99) argues that the weaving together of sacrifice and economy constitutes a system of sacrificonomics, demonstrating the case that in the US, prisons are the basis of state economies providing industry and employment. This is increasingly the case for the UK with for example the Ministry of Justice announcing a prison building programme for 10, 000 new places, 'to boost rehabilitation and support the economy' (https://www.gov.uk/government/news/four-new-prisons-boost-rehabilitation-and-support-economy). Runions (2021: 99) argues that the sacrificial violence, governance, conquest and control operating in prisons as a form of racial and colonial conquest (and an extension of slavery) is where 'salvific payment ominously mimics imperializing economic violence and the extension of power'. Further, prison (or probation) does not free people from their debt to society but perpetuates control through assent to rehabilitation with the annexation of docile bodies, mainly through labour; a conquest rather than a liberation. Singh (2021) observes that broadly speaking the history of financialization is the history of Christianity, and that the prison-industrial complex is a clear example of the merging of sacrifice and debt logics. He argues (using a Foucauldian analysis) that prison ministries that focus on helping the prisoner to bear the punishment are a microcosm of the larger project of mass incarceration, where redeeming scapegoats as exploited labour generate surpluses for society under the guise of repaying their own debts.

The communities of scapegoats carry society; this is their sacrificial function. Rather than healing harms we use the innocence of the victim to justify the creation of new victims based on their guilt and promise them rehabilitation, which is not and cannot be delivered through current penal logic. Jesus understood that sacrificonomics were located in time and space, which in the case of the Temple was the court of the Gentiles. The moneylenders who provided for legitimate pilgrims to convert currency had located themselves in the only place that people outside of the Hebrew covenant could experience the grace of God. This identifies the great crime of criminal justice, that the invitation to a space of rehabilitation is blocked by economic, self-interested and sacrificial demands.

The powerlessness paradox

Singh (2021) raises the question of how constructive interventions that challenge colonial, Eurocentric and white supremacist categories of thought in criminal justice, and that model and affirm the new, might look. The archaic sacrificial builds communities and social order around the scapegoat, but as we discussed in Chapter 3, the execution of Jesus of Nazareth changed the rules of the game and ushered in the modern age. However, the scapegoated innocent cannot use their innocence to pursue and defeat their oppressor. In the words of Jesus, '[i]f Satan casts out Satan, he is divided against himself; how then will his kingdom stand?' (Matthew 12: 26).

Satan cannot cast out Satan; you cannot go after people by using the scapegoating thesis, otherwise you are already within the shadow of their mimetic desire and they become a rival and thus violence is perpetuated (see Girard, 2001). The actions of Jesus in the Temple demonstrate that he did not attack the people themselves but expelled the objects of their acquisitive mimesis – the trade in animals and money that prevented access to grace. In so doing, he asked them to focus on the true purpose of the Temple as the house of God, and so Matthew (21: 14) states that after cleansing the Temple '[t]he blind and the lame came to him in the temple, and he cured them;' by placing these activities in the court of the Gentiles, this becomes a mission to all. The text restores the meaning of what is holy through revealing the violent sacred. This revelation requires a giving up of reprisals and an embracing of powerlessness, which has no immediate and tangible benefits. As Girard (1978) argues, a peace surpassing human understanding can only be found on the other side of our desire for justice and judgement, and likewise Millbank (2006) argues that this Gospel is completely distinct from self-assertion, rivalry and the subtracting of something from others. We need then to understand not just the theory but also the practice of bearing each other's burdens, as our primary choice, rather than our choice being one of condemnation. Pauline theology challenges the world through organizations such as AA as it 'justifies the formation of norm-violating communities, while his [Paul's] missionary practice clarifies and radicalizes the incongruity of the gift of Christ' (Barclay, 2015: 567).

Desire for the second death

In stark contrast, the concept of Hell, eternal damnation, a second death is a core onto-theological construct of punishment. The object of desire is a conceptualization of an ongoing metaphysical punishment, even for those executed, and this is evident in the Puritan theologies of the founding fathers of the US. As Van Wormer and Starks (2012: 157) argue, '[i]n our view, religiously defined notions of morality, which are conservative in nature, are the overriding factor that sets the US apart from other western nations. This moralistic ethos … lies in the very foundation of American history.'

The Trump presidency in its last months between July 2020 and January 2021 carried out 13 federal executions, against precedent (https://www. bbc.co.uk/news/world-us-canada-55236260). Clearly, there was a political hope that the spectacle of the sacred sacrificial could invigorate voters and through this theatre instil the Presidency with new life for another four years. The work of Christopher Bracken (2018) provides a case study into the dynamics of the New England settlers and the use of the death penalty to assert sovereignty over the indigenous people. In 1772 the person to be executed was Moses Paul, a Native American, and Bracken states (2018: 8): 'If Paul were to die both temporally and eternally, he would fulfill the genocidal fantasies of those who desire the death of "the Indian nations." In executing him, the sovereign is exterminating competing sovereignties.'

Derrida (cited in Bracken, 2018) argues that the sovereign not only condemns, but also forgives (see Chapter 3) and is a power that gives itself its own law, with an indivisibility based upon a fantasy of immunity. This strong sovereignty exercises condemnation and forgiveness but is accountable to no other processes, except a transcendent sovereign, who justifies metaphysical violence grounded in the sacred sacrificial.

John Caputo (2006, cited in Bracken, 2018) indicates that in the New Testament Paul entertains two versions of God: one who is strong, '[l]et every person be subject to the governing authorities; for there is no authority except from God, and those authorities that exist have been instituted by God' (Romans 13: 1); and the other who 'chose what is foolish in the world to shame the wise; God chose what is weak in the world to shame the strong; God chose what is low and despised in the world, things that are not, to reduce to nothing things that are' (1 Corinthians: 1–29). Paul's weak sovereign undermines and divides the sovereignty of the sacred sacrificial through the revelation of the crucifixion of Jesus (Paul's whole gospel is Christ crucified). In the words of Caputo (cited in Bracken, 2018: 12), '[t]he kingdom calls the world out'. In calling the world out and in denying the death penalty, it is, for Derrida, the possibility of the gift of the other who appeals for grace and pardon against the condemnation that gives me life. This other is not transcendent or metaphysical but stands before me with an unconditional gift of forgiveness that is an obligation to preserve life. The teaching of the Catholic Church has changed to reflect this position: 'today capital punishment is unacceptable, however serious the condemned's crime may have been … no matter how serious the crime that has been committed, the death penalty is inadmissible because it is an attack on the inviolability and dignity of the person' (Francis, 2015). This developing position by the Roman Catholic Church on capital punishment demonstrates the importance of having a tradition that can rectify both historical problems and errors that have emerged (see, for example, MacIntyre, 1990). This can allow us to dismantle the tradition of harsh punishments underpinned by Christian theology. With respect to capital punishment, Catholic judges on the US Supreme Court and politicians can no longer rely on Church teaching to support the death penalty and harsh penal measures. These changes have coincided with an increased understanding of universal salvation as opposed to the 'metaphysical whips of Hell' (see the discussion on Bloch in Chapter 2) which underpin the criminal justice system.

Holy Saturday

The desire of rehabilitation ostensibly is to address the ills of society that both cause and perpetuate crime. We argue throughout this book that rehabilitation fails by the terms of its own logic through perpetuating scapegoats who are of economic value to wider society. Society applauds the successes of rehabilitation, but they are the exceptions that prove the rule of the institutional failures of justice. In Christian tradition, following his death and prior to his resurrection, Jesus descended into Hell, providing us with a model for practice in criminal justice. What is at stake here through redemption is new life, which follows the event of crime. The Biblical mythos is as silent as Jesus' grave concerning what happens until the resurrection on Easter Sunday. After all, what can possibly happen to or with Jesus' condemned, docile, powerless and completely dead body? But even in death he is obedient to God's redemptive mission and

> [t]akes the existential measure of everything that is sheerly contrary to God ... But at the same time this happening gives the measure of the Father's mission in all its amplitude: the 'exploration' of Hell is an event of the Trinity ... the Son must 'take in with his own eyes what in the realm of creation is imperfect, unformed, chaotic' so as to make it pass over into his domain as the Redeemer ... His exploration of the ultimate depths has transformed what was a prison into a way. (Von Balthasar, 1990: 175)

Holy Saturday marks the necessary death of metaphysical punishment as Christ's flesh (*sarx* – see Chapter 5) is carried by the Father and the Holy Spirit to be one with the condemned, but not be left there. The Father who has unjustly lost his Son to violence of the mob, whipped up by religious leaders and politicians, takes being with the dead as the point of departure for new life (see Von Balthasar, 1990). From this moment of departure, Christ carries Hell in his heart and communicates its reality to us, and calls us like him to bear witness to his harrowing of it. Called to enter into the hell of other people's experiences, we rescue them from it, rather than leaving our scapegoated sacrificial victims as the food for our own demonic compulsions.

Easter Sunday and beyond

The hermeneutical truth revealed in the sacrifice, death and resurrection of Jesus is that redemption is universal and the responsibility of each one of us. Every sin, misdemeanour and crime is forgivable, and despite the difficulties of this and its significance, it is our responsibility to try to find a way to do so. Of hermeneutical significance is that the resurrection of this dead man was not at the end of time (whether the time of physics or God's time), but an interruption of our own personal time, and thus significant to each of us as individuals. As an example, Saul, the man complicit in murder (see Chapter 5), was a witness to the resurrected Jesus. This complicity was not an impediment to redemption but would appear to be a prerequisite, as compared to the close followers of Jesus (his Apostles), who did not appear to understand what was going on, and for which he frequently upbraided them. This resurrection for the Judaism of its time was unheard of and for Hellenist thought could only be something far off in the future. Between the chronology of life and death is the paradox of new life actualized, with Jesus actively choosing (calling) those who had betrayed him to promote this reality.

The Gospel of John (21: 1–19) narrates an event that happened after the resurrection when Jesus forgives Peter for betraying him. Jesus cooked breakfast on the beach of the Sea of Tiberias for a number of the disciples who had decided to return to their previous lives as fishermen. When captured by the Temple Guard, his followers abandoned Jesus, with Peter denying three times that he knew him. The return to fishing was a further betrayal as it was a clear indication that the people involved were going to carry on as if the whole 'Jesus experience' was over. The narrative demonstrates that this choice was futile as they caught nothing until someone shouted from the shore to drop their nets on the other side of the boat, which they did, and the nets were full. It was only at this point that they recognized the person on the shore as Jesus. He had bread and fish cooking over a brazier and he invited the others to bring their fish too, and provided them with breakfast; he added to what they already had and they realized it was Jesus but were too afraid to ask. The hermeneutic is that of the inauguration of the Kingdom of God, which is always a plus, plus (superabundance and incongruity of the gift). The brazier is symbolic of that around which Peter sat when he denied and betrayed Jesus and which now provides sustenance to the undeserving:

When they had eaten, Jesus said to Simon Peter, 'Simon son of John, do you love me more than these others do?' He answered 'Yes, Lord, you know I love you.' Jesus said to him, 'Feed my lambs.' A second time he said to him, 'Simon son of John, do you love me?' He replied 'Yes, Lord, you know I love you,' Jesus said to him, 'Look after my sheep.' Then he said to him a third time, 'Simon son of John, do you love me?' Peter was hurt that he asked him a third time, 'Do you love me?' and said, 'Lord you know everything; you know I love you.' Jesus said to him, 'Feed my sheep.'

Jesus does not respond to his betrayal and denial with denunciation, and a demanding of apology and recompense, but rather with an affirmation that a wrong has been committed, and that something good can come of it. The gift of a real meal opens up the space, with the energy and the matter both entwined (see Chapter 2) as the basis for this dialogue. This enables Jesus' companions, who are failures in the eyes of the world, to set out on their mission. Further, the model is one of understanding the need to invite ourselves into other people's lives and to provide the necessary assistance when they are too afraid to ask us or or cannot provide for themselves.

The Redemptive Practitioner

Redemption is an active process that engages with the dynamic nature of reality and its entanglement of energies. Through being a person-for-others (see later), and the making of ethical choices the redemptive practitioner transubstantiates (see later) matter. The redemptive practitioner is a conjunctive (not disjunctive and separate) part of the unfolding and meeting of the trajectories of past, present and future, enabling an articulation, visualization and actualization of the person as they are in themself and for others, whether having been designated criminal or victim. This seeks to heal the harms wrought by the catastrophic violation of individuals, families and communities that is criminal justice in the UK and US. These harms represent the failures of the utilitarian processes of disjunction and reductionism, the metaphysics of deontology and the elitism of virtue ethics. For Dietrich Bonhoeffer these philosophical frameworks as *cor incurvum in se* (Latin: the heart turned in on itself) allow no room for radical and real otherness (Clements, 2000). This is a development on the theology and ethics of Karl Barth, which challenges individualistic ideas of morality, held by economically and privileged Christians (or systems and organizations founded in Christianity) who attempt to exonerate themselves from complicity in social sin and injustice (McBride and Fabisiak, 2020).

As a matter of urgency criminal justice, practice and its underpinning criminology, theology and philosophy need to focus at the level of the individual practitioner and their resources for ethical and normative practice as the dynamics of change come from the bottom up (see Chapter 1). For Bonhoeffer this practice is one of freedom not from others, but for others, precisely as God acts towards us (McBride and Fabisiak, 2020). The ways in which we teach and train practitioners is fundamental, not least because reductionism into separate disciplinary silos means that many resources remain hidden from each other, or treated with suspicion. In part, the hermeneutical narrative of this book is an attempt to realize new perspectives across 'science' and 'humanities'. Of importance is the ways in which practitioners interpret their own lives within the context of the processes and institutions of justice for example as a practitioner within the criminal justice system what are the sources of the self that are used in interpreting and creating a biographical narrative in engaging in that work? How do the criminal justice system and the individual practitioner mutually interpret each other? In the face of a totalizing metaphysic of punishment and retribution how do I begin to ask these questions and then how do I act dependent upon the answer? This book has sought to provide some of those resources and narratives and in way that overcomes the false divides created by the Cartesian and Newtonian understanding of the clockwork, mechanical and disjunctive universe (see Chapter 2).

Bonheoffer's New Theology

Bonhoeffer was a Lutheran pastor who during the 1930s helped to set up the Confessing Church to counter the attempts by the Nazi government to establish one pro-Nazi Protestant and evangelical Church. Although a pacifist, he later became involved in a plot to assassinate Adolf Hitler. His New Theology based on 'the nonreligious interpretation of biblical terms in world come of age' was Bonhoeffer's re-evaluation of his theology when imprisoned by the Nazis, and in the final year of his life before execution (Bethge, 2000). Bonhoeffer's theology is instructive in shining a light on the relationship between individuals (creativity) and institutions (conformity) that has existed at least since the Edict of Milan in 313 CE. In this edict the Roman Emperor Constantine paved the way for Christianity to become the state religion, but in the name, primarily, of public welfare, security and the good of the state. Thus, through legitimizing Christianity, an institutional Church intimately entwined with the state, and the maintenance of social order through punishment began to evolve (see Chapter 4) based on the sacred sacrificial (see Chapter 6). Agamben (2011) sees the development of the government machine as based in ancient Greek and early Christian understandings of *oikonomia* (Gr: economy. Lit. Household management – memories here of Margaret Thatcher suggesting that running the country was no different to running a household) as a theological articulation between the Kingdom of God and government, effective management and ceremonial and liturgical functions. Agamben develops the Foucauldian concept of spectacle and the concept of glory as the defining link between *oikonomia* and government, political apparatuses and democracy, arguing that in a so-called post-religious age the media and their power come from dispensing glory through acclamation and doxology. It is useful to consider here the importance of post-trial statements via the media by victims of crime (see Chapter 3) and prosecutors. With serious crimes, explicitly theological terms such as 'truly evil', 'beyond redemption' and so on are a part of a deliberate strategy of *enargeia*, 'the "vivid" quality of language that encourages listeners or readers to develop mental images' (O'Connell, 2017: 225) and thus (even through the best intentions to do good) become spectators and partakers of a communion of virtual and metaphysical violence.

In seeking the sources of governmentality in *oikonomia*, Agamben (2011) sees this as distinctly Trinitarian, in so far as governance is modelled on working out how Jesus as the son of the Father is his delegated representative on earth while remaining co-equal in divinity and power with him and the Holy Spirit (Singh, 2018). Marion Grau (2004) argues that the structures of divine economy maintain structures of hierarchy, dominance and control, and for Agamben (2011) the locus of this control is to be found in the office of the priesthood and the operation of the sacred mystery of the Mass.

The meaning of the Mass as the Eucharistic meal (see later) was central to the reformations that occurred in the western Church (Latin rite) between 1490 and 1700 CE (see MacCulloch, 2003 for a definitive history), leading to the formation of the Protestant Churches as distinct from (what became) the Roman Catholic Church. Particularly, 'Agamben sees the way in which the priest's operation of the sacred mystery of the Mass depends on his office and not his person as an antecedent to the valorization of impersonal duty (*officio*) in modern ethics' (Yoder, 2020: 1).

The theology of Bonhoeffer, emerging from the Second World War and the realities of the Holocaust, addresses the subjective in a process of redemption. The experiences of large sections of the Christian Churches in Germany becoming complicit in Nazism Bonhoeffer saw as stupidity, where people simply chose to abdicate responsibility rather than actively choosing to engage in crimes against humanity. Bonhoeffer understood that stupidity is not overcome by force or persuasion and that only an act of divine forgiveness first could change people's lives (von Kellenbach, 2013). Repentance follows from the intervention of forgiveness, and its necessity based on the understanding that no amount of atonement can give satisfaction for a wrong done, especially with respect to serious crime (see Chapter 3).

For Bonhoeffer academic theology for its own sake is meaningless and unfaithful to God, rather there is a need to engage with the reality of lived experience (McBride, 2014), not metaphysical categories of thought. In this sense, he rejected pietism and its failure to engage with the world, the Church as making concrete God's revelation, and the problem of the Church (including his own anti-Nazi Confessing Church) as promoting itself (engaging in conservative restoration rather than revealing truth) rather than being towards the world (Lenehan, 2010). Bonhoeffer's radical and outrageous demand is that we give up trying to be or to do good as when we assume a moral, pious or religious position apropos another then we situate ourselves as equal to God and thus superior to the other and condemning them to dehumanization and violence. Like Nietzsche, Bonhoeffer calls for a transvaluation of all values, but unlike Nietzsche bases this call on an understanding of Christ for the world. McBride and Fabisiak (2020: 13) state the importance of this theology in relation to criminal justice thus:

> To begin to imagine human beings as created to be 'free for others,' then, can awaken us to forms of justice grounded in

responsibility and in the interdependence of human life. Such an orientation opposes the foundational lie of the carceral system: that we can be free from violence and harm by finding and condemning bad people. It demands instead that we recognize all of our complicity in the social order, and that we take responsibility for the human world and lives of others. And this leads to other ways of doing justice.

The Protestant vision derived from Luther is not one of detached and impersonal duty, but it was precisely impersonal duty that drove the Holocaust, as

> [b]y and large, perpetrators of atrocities do not torture and kill for personal gain or satisfaction, and they try hard not to break the law. In general, they do not lose control over their desires and succumb to envy, lust, greed or anger. Rather they enforce the law and they actively deny personal moral agency and claim ignorance, impotence and dependence. (von Kellenbach, 2013: 18)

In this sense, the philosopher Max Picard (Picard and Hauser, 2010) conceives of Adolf Hitler as a post office clerk running down the road, to give a customer the change back that they had left on the counter. Picard's understanding of the 'Hitler in each one of us', then, requires each one of us to evaluate our moral agency both as individuals and as people who constitute society, civic society and organizations. Bonhoeffer in his New Theology critiques philosophical ethics and returns us to an examination of theological ethics, as does Paul Ricoeur in his phrase 'the economy of gift' (see Wall, 2001: 235 and Chapter 6). Through theological ethics we can examine, understand and address the problems of complicity in systems of racialized evil, whether the Third Reich or the modern use of mass incarceration. The great African American theologian of liberation James Cone (2017: 155) states it thus:

> [T]he Christian gospel is more than a transcendent reality, more than 'going to heaven when I die to shout salvation as I fly'. It is also an immanent reality – a powerful liberating presence among the poor right *now* in their midst, 'building them up when they are torn down and propping them up on the leaning side.' The gospel is found wherever poor people struggle for justice, fighting for their right to life, liberty and the pursuit of happiness. Bee Jenkins' claims that 'Jesus won't fail you' was made in the heat of the struggle for civil rights in Mississippi, and such faith gave her strength and courage to fight for justice against overwhelming

odds. Without concrete signs of divine presence in the lives of the poor, the gospel becomes simply an opiate; rather than liberating the powerless from humiliation and suffering, the gospel becomes a drug that helps them adjust to this world by looking for 'pie in the sky'. And so the transcendent and immanent, heaven and earth, must be held together in critical, dialectical tension, each one correcting the limits of the other. (emphasis in the original)

The catastrophe of our age is that the places of justice are places of injustice, obscured by appeals to reason (see Pycroft, 2021b). These forms of 'reason' are stupidity and banality, neither of which can be justified, whereas the gift of grace is precisely that of justification for those who, in the eyes of 'the world', should not be justified.

The active probation officer

Building on Bonhoeffer, our hermeneutical narrative focuses on the potential for redemption being in the embodied presence, will and actions of the criminal justice practitioner, which occupies liminal space. This space and its narrative are always a choice made by the individual in learning, dialogue and storytelling with the other and others (see later). It is therefore partial, unfinalized and open ended but oriented by a commitment to being, becoming and actualizing. The word 'parole' is derived from the French for 'word' and specifically relates to *parole d'honneur*, a word of honour given under oath. The French is a derivation from the Greek *parabola*, meaning 'to speak', linked to parables and storytelling. The word 'probation' is from the Latin *probare*, meaning to test or prove. 'Approbation' (Latin: *aprobare* – lit. 'to assent to') would follow from finding that something is good, or 'disapprobation' if not. 'Probation' is not an active noun whereas both 'approbation' and 'disapprobation' are.

The Probation Service in England and Wales originated as a theological enterprise and was intended as an opportunity for people to demonstrate good behaviour, and for the criminal justice system to exercise mercy, where and when possible (Burke, 2021). Probation was an alternative to punishment, with punishment only following if the faith that the courts placed in the individual was not reciprocated. However, the practices of probation, since the 1970s, have been assimilated into the punitive turn in criminal justice. In England and Wales in 1996 the then Home Secretary took the decision that probation officers should no longer be trained as social workers as this was seen as being soft on crime. In 1997 the incoming New Labour government took the decision that probation officers should have degrees in criminology (this position remains). In answer to the question of what criminology, they could only have been thinking of 'administrative criminology', the term coined by Jock Young (2012) to describe positivist research in the British Home Office based upon Martinson's 'nothing works' research (Martinson, 1974). This approach was to reduce opportunities for offending, while incarcerating those who did offend. The role of criminologists was to evaluate the effectiveness of those approaches. Young describes these approaches as '[a] detachment of individuals from the social structure, a denial of history, a loss of meaning; it forgoes transformative politics and concentrates on amelioration and accommodation to the status quo' (Young, 2012: 427). Probation officers were intended to become objective technocrats, assessing and managing risk, manipulating resources between community and prison, and with commensurate bureaucratic responsibilities.

In England and Wales, community sentences are now a punishment in their own right and consequently there has never been greater distance between the individual practitioner and the people they are 'supervising' (an apt word that denotes a fundamental hierarchy and distance between the supervisor and supervisee). In seeking to close this gap our approach is focused on the individual practitioner through an examination of connectedness as an ontological reality that provides a 'ground of being' in an implicate order (theorized by David Bohm – Chapter 2). This order is dynamic and evolutionary in nature (as adumbrated by complexity theory – Chapter 2), and culturally revealed in Girard's concept of the violent and the sacred (Chapter 4). In an age of insecurity and hyper-individualism, communication is through the perceived guilt of the scapegoat, upon which all agree, with both the political left and right trying to outbid each other on who can be toughest on crime. Each side, faction, group feel completely justified in their arguments. However, due to their similarities they cannot see their unanimity that generates failure and violence.

An active probation officer committed to being and actualization opens a space of possibility through loving kindness (*hesed* – see Chapter 3), discernment and testing, and the thinking of the impossible (see later). Being able to see if something is true, and the impossibility of its truth, is a key biblical message, achieved by having a face towards and for the other, where truth is revealed in the construction of this relationship – this is 'the thing in itself' of probation, its haecceity. The Greek *dokimazō*, related to the noun *dokime*, means what is accepted (dogma), with the verb *dokeo* meaning to mentally accept, thus invoking images that refer to observable reality. The related noun *dokos* describes the main beam that is supporting either the roof or floor of a building. In the New Testament, *dokimazō* means to interpret, to evaluate, to test, to examine, to discern and to approve. The probation officer is thus supporting and en-fleshing change, through the for-giving of the material necessities of being, living and flourishing as a human being.

This 'for the other' is always a multiplicity in unity of undivided wholeness in flowing movement (see Chapter 2), for the criminal, for the victim and for the community. We have already discussed Christie's conflicts as property argument (Chapter 4) and problems of similarity through bureaucratization. We can add to this surveillance as control, the use of electronic tagging and monitoring through telephone calls rather than face-to-face, therapeutically informed interventions (see Arrigo and Sellers, 2021). Some probation services in England and Wales are employing people to complete risk assessments on offenders and they do so without actually meeting the individual offender. This reduction of relationship to purely transactional information sets perpetuates the virtual as non-being, rather than consummating being. In the same way that habeas corpus is a key doctrine for the criminal courts, then the same principle needs to apply to criminal justice interventions where both the worker and the offender have a physical presence to each other. Because the concept of 'the good' has become so bound up with the will and reason in our Cartesian and Kantian world, the body and its needs have become a secondary consideration. St Paul makes clear that both the spirit and the body receive new life as a consequence of the resurrection of Christ (Romans 8: 10–11).

Truth from the heart

Non-violent mutuality and empowerment is truth. At the trial of Jesus of Nazareth, the Roman Governor Pontius Pilate understood the truth but nonetheless was willing to convict an innocent man to maintain social order. If he did not then the truth was also that he might lose his own life as punishment for the loss of social order and an affront to imperial power. Under questioning from Pilate, Jesus says:

> I came into this world for this, to bear witness to the truth; and all who are on the side of truth listens to my voice. 'Truth' said Pilate. 'What is that?' And so saying he went out again to the Jews and said, 'I find no case against him. But according to a custom of yours I should release one prisoner at the Passover; would you like me then, to release for you the king of the Jews?' At this, they shouted. 'Not this man but Barabbas.' Barabbas was a bandit. (John 18: 38–40)

To paraphrase Bonhoeffer, the truth that both shames and heartens us is to be a man or woman for others. This is the individual practitioner calling out the sacred sacrificial of neoliberal capitalism, bureaucratic rationalism, competition and marketization, which are indifferent to morality and reform (see Whitehead, 2018). The scapegoat mechanism reveals that the myths and rituals of violence and sacrifice (re)produce state and society, with the mechanisms of justice as bloodstained feedback loops fundamental to social order. Rehabilitation perpetuates these myths. The criminal justice practitioner needs to examine and renounce their own violence but requires a frame of reference within which to understand themself and the work that they do. This cannot be reduced to a day's training on unconscious bias. It is hard to disagree with Bill Michael, who had to resign from KPMG after saying that '[a]fter every single unconscious bias training that's ever been done nothing's ever improved. So unless you care, you actually won't change' (https://www.spectator.co.uk/article/why-unconscious-bias-train ing-doesn-t-work). This training may be a starting point but the reality of police violence and institutional racism in the US and UK are testament to its pervasiveness. It is necessary to constantly ask colleagues and service users the extent to which I/we are complicit in the dynamics of scapegoating, particularly where there are agreement, consensus and, in legal cases, unanimous verdicts against individuals, which are taken as a good thing because this indicates little room for doubt. The organizations and teams that we work in can all agree on the relative merits of particular individuals or groups of people. However, in the Talmud (the Jewish law) we find a remarkable statement:

> R[abbi] Kahana said: If the Sanhedrin [Jewish court] unanimously find [the accused] guilty, he is acquitted. Why? – Because we have learned by tradition that sentence must be postponed till the morrow in hope of finding new points in favor of the defense. But this cannot be anticipated in this case. (cited by Glatt, 2013: 322)

There is extensive debate concerning the meaning of this paradoxical statement, with Glatt (2013) offering the following observations. First, the 19th-century scholar Zvi Hirsh Chajes argues that it is the role of the Sanhedrin to make an impossible argument, particularly because in the face of a lack of dissenting opinion, collusion must be suspected; hence, they are not doing their job properly as they are not making the impossible arguments, and the charge should be dismissed. In fact, the basis for admission to the Sanhedrin is the ability to provide 'a cogent, logical argument for an impossible factual scenario. The judge must prove that a certain dead animal, ritually impure according to the explicit text of the Bible, is actually ritually pure according to Jewish law' (Glatt, 2013: 324). Likewise, in the 16th century Judah Loew argued that the role of the Sanhedrin is to search for evidence of innocence rather than guilt, and to be committed to finding merit in the defendant rather than being concerned with punishment. For Loew the integrity of the court as one of righteousness that frees rather than punishes innocent people is the priority (this is a statement of the priority of due process models of justice). There are further views concerning the nature of punishment as being spiritually cleansing, with Menachem Mendel Morgenstern arguing that punishment is the mode of forgiveness. In this approach, the role of the Sanhedrin is to help a person to realize that they have done wrong and to regret their actions. A unanimous verdict would bring about this understanding to the offender, obviating the need for punishment.

Antoni Mikulski

Aaron Pycroft has the privilege and pleasure of Toni's friendship after having worked with him both in the Probation Service and at Portsmouth University. Placed on probation in the late 1960s when probation was a social work-oriented organization, he went on to become a senior probation officer in the 1990s and thus his experiences provide an interesting reflection on changes in probation practice. By the end of the 1990s probation was committing itself to the 'what works' and public protection agendas (see Nash and Williams, 2008), with a dominant risk agenda leading to the abandonment of a social work ethos. The focus on 'dangerous offenders' led to the creation of Multi-Agency Public Protection Arrangements, which Toni was responsible for coordinating in Portsmouth.

Toni's mother had died in his early teens and his father's work commitments meant that Toni had very little parental oversight. He was convicted of 'aiding and abetting taking and driving away' (nowadays known as taking without consent) as there was no intent to permanently deprive the owner of the car (these were always returned) and a probation order ensued. Toni's experience of probation revolves around his relationship with his supervising officer, who, through an immediacy of response, provided a framework which gave security and confidence. This always included asking Toni's employment status and if necessary making phone calls to secure him a job. However, while on probation, Toni, drinking in the pubs of Portsmouth, would often get into fights, and on one such occasion a police officer reflected on the fact that in the last few fights he had dealt with Toni was always involved. What the police officer then did changed Toni's life. He suggested that Toni should join a boxing club, which he did, and he went on to become a professional boxer, ranked number three in the UK. When he retired from boxing, Toni eventually trained as a probation officer and psychotherapist and became an academic involved in qualifying probation officers. He then became director of a prison-based therapeutic community. He is clear that current bureaucratized probation (or police) practice and the focus on future risk would not have assisted him in developing a meaningful life due to the closing down or prevention of opportunities. It was the fact of people taking an interest in him through both initiating a new virtual narrative but also providing the necessary resources to actualize his immediate needs that enabled him to become who he was.

Facing the other

This story demonstrates the importance of others having an ability to perceive through empathy and intuition the sparks of possibility that Jankélévitch (2005) relates to a creative and generative principle based on 'giving that which one is not' (2005: xvii). In overcoming the judicial and social dynamics of scapegoating, to be a paraclete means to have a face and a heart for the other (see later).

Levinas' ontology (or ethics as first philosophy) sees that face as revealing the fragility of the person and their exposure, their uniqueness and history. For Levinas the other becomes the transcendent I (they are an epiphany for me), an ultimate and exorbitant encounter with others' meaning and value, that returns us to understanding the image of God (*eikon* or *icon* – see Chapter 6) rather than reducing our focus to the reason and rationality of human beings that is expressed in the European philosophical tradition (Moore, 2010). The face reveals rather than obscures the truth, as recalled in the maxim 'the camera never lies' (at least pre-Photoshop). Camus (1988: 18) argues that '[i]t is certain that apparently though I have seen the actor a hundred times, I shall not for that reason know him any better personally'. Camus eventually rebels against this gap with the other (the gap is expressed also in his novel *The Stranger* (Camus, 1989)), through a humanist commitment to that other (as expressed in his novel *The Plague* (Camus, 2002)) and philosophy developed in *The Rebel* (Camus, 2000). The publication of the latter led to Camus' rejection by the Sartrean left – see Chapter 4). This commitment, which Levinas expresses as obligation, the infinite command of the other, known phenomenologically through intuition and empathy, reveals truth. The space between two people (between two faces) becomes the space of creativity.

John

John provides a useful illustration of how a moment within a therapeutic intervention can change a self-narrative. John was articulate, funny, a great storyteller and a skilled wood worker. He came from one of the poorest parts of Liverpool and was alcohol dependent. I (Aaron Pycroft) started working with him in 1989 when he was in supported accommodation and oversaw his transition into independent accommodation. He continued in this accommodation and was a regular user of the workshop facilities provided, and was relatively stable with respect to his drinking and drug use. A number of years later he came to see me as his drinking was becoming problematic and his mental health deteriorating. We agreed that he would join one of our residential programmes. This six-week programme was predominantly a group work intervention that I had developed, utilizing approaches to cognitive behavioural interventions within a group process approach (also many of the participants attended AA as well). John completed the programme and returned home, and then a couple of years later was successful in applying for a job as a substance misuse worker in our detoxification centre. In conversation I asked John what had contributed to the stability in his life and he referenced a particular group work activity. In this group, each person lay down on sheets of paper to allow a full-size outline of themselves to be drawn by another. They then had to populate their outline with their key qualities and positive characteristics. The images of the self for the whole group were then pinned on the wall around the outside of the group, 'looking in'. John says that by having the experience of his positive self looking at himself in the here and now, it powerfully disrupted the self-narrative of how he had previously viewed himself.

The dynamics of a group constructed as a therapeutic intervention, within a service and a wider organization (this can be extrapolated further), has a multitude of faces. Levinas' (1969) introduction of the Third is an understanding that the ego has to respond to more than one other in social situations (and thus moves Levinas' thought into the realm of justice and politics – Simmons, 1999). It is useful here to use Lacan's concept of other (with lower case o) and Other (with upper case O). Lacan speaks of the individual ego as other, thus indicating its alien status from myself. However, the other may also be seen as an alter ego, an imaginary, a transference of how I would like to be. The Other is of two types. First, big-Other constitutes the symbolic order of language and cultural negotiations constituting interpersonal relationships, which in the case of John can refer to the group process negotiated and agreed by its members, but can also be authoritative and impersonal power (Johnston, 2018) for example the requirements of the wider organization, or a court order. Second, big-Other refers to that which is real in the sense of being outside the symbolic order; it is no longer virtual and exists within a material sense. Therapeutically, transference relationships (which are predominantly the recapitulation of the primary family experience – see Yalom, 2021) are virtual and not real in the sense that they remain symbolic. Greenson (1967, cited in Watkins, 2011: 102) says:

> The term 'real' in the 'real relationship' may mean realistic, reality oriented, or undistorted as contrasted to the term 'transference,' which connotes unrealistic, distorted and inappropriate. The word real may also refer to genuine, authentic, true in contrast to artificial, synthetic or assumed. At this point, I intend to use the term real to refer to the realistic and genuine relationship between analyst and patient.

In the case of John, the virtual appearance of himself to himself (as *icon*) had actualized himself. The Thirds have enabled the exorbitant demand of John's face to be for himself, and within the context of this group, to be for others too. This plus, plus (superabundance and incongruity), given and giving, the economy of grace in action, requires no scapegoat or bloody sacrifice.

In Judeo-Christian theology the Holy Spirit is the breath and creative (poetic) energy (*dunamis*) of God, the paraclete (Gr: *paráklētos*), the truth that is the creative relationship between the Father and the Son in their soteriological mission. The Hebrew for spirit is *rūaḥ*, a feminine designation (whereas in Greek *pneûma* is neuter, and Latin *spiritus* is male), a legal advocate or counsel for the defence. In Judaism a good deed was called a paraclete or advocate, and a transgression was an accuser. Repentance and good works were called paracletes: 'The works of benevolence and mercy done by the people of Israel in this world become agents of peace and intercessors (paracletes) between them and their Father in heaven.' The sin offering is a paraclete; the paraclete created by each good deed is called an angel' (Jewish Encyclopedia, IX, 514–15, article 'Paraclete').

In Judaism and early Christianity, Satan, rather than having a being, is, through accusation (French: *j'accuse*), hindrance or temptation, the illusory obstacle to *tikkun olam* (Hebrew: repairing the world) and the overcoming of idolatry (https://www.jewishvirtuallibrary.org/satan). Also, Stokes (2014) shows from the biblical evidence that the noun *śāṭān* (transliteration from the Hebrew) relates specifically to physical attack. In this sense, another person can be my *śāṭān* or I can be a *śāṭān* to another person. The scapegoating mechanism, and the metaphysical and collective violence of all against the one, to resolve communal crises is in this sense, and the sense in which Jesus identified it, is satanic (see Chapter 4). This why Jesus says:

> Come to terms with your opponent in good time while you are still on your way to the court with him, or he may hand you over to the judge and the judge to the officer, and you will be thrown into prison. In truth I tell you, you will not get out till you have paid the last penny. (Matthew 5: 25–26)

This contrasts with the metaphysics of Greek thought where Poena is the Goddess of punishment and vengeance whose consort is Tartarus. Tartarus is both a deity (the offspring of Gaia and Chaos, existing before the Olympian Gods) and a place of punishment (Hell, Hades). There is no escape from punishment except in the capricious will of the Gods, whereas Jesus places for-giveness and release in the hands of each one of us. This exorbitant invitation by the face of Christ to forgive the other and to demonstrate radical equality is truly terrifying at a human level.

Law and violence

In the psychoanalysis of Lacan (2019), for example, truth is always the movement and the search for truth between two or more people and does not emerge in any absolute sense. However, in speaking truth to power it is necessary to reveal the violence of the law in interpreting its retributive and rehabilitative functions, Robert Gibbs (2006) develops the ethics of Levinas with the legal theory of Robert Cover (Minow et al, 1995) to examine the ethics of the courtroom. This development within a framework of hermeneutical phenomenology provides useful insights for probation (and other criminal justice) practice, with respect to the demands that the face of the other places upon me. Gibbs' approach helps us to understand probation practice and the interpretation of law as ambiguity and tension with a chiasmic[1] (reversible) structure between punishment and rehabilitation, justice and mercy, criminal and victim. An understanding of this chiasm enables us to appreciate specific roles within the practices of justice and how the probation officer, through practice, may demonstrate love and mercy towards the other in the face of institutional violence.

Cover (1995: 203) states that

> [l]egal interpretation takes place in a field of pain and death ... Legal interpretive acts signal and occasion the imposition of violence upon others: A judge articulates her understanding of a text, and as a result, somebody loses his freedom, his property, his children, even his life. Interpretations in law also constitute justifications of violence which has already occurred or is about to occur. When interpreters have finished their work, they frequently leave behind victims whose lives have been torn apart by these organized, social practices of violence. Neither legal interpretation nor the violence it occasions may be properly understood apart from one another.

The tough-on-crime rhetoric, common to the US and UK since the 1970s, includes the argument that probation is a soft option (see Kaye and Gibbs, 2010 in the UK context), and that if we use community sentences as being economically expedient then we need to ensure that those sentences are as tough as prison sentences. As Hal Pepinsky (2006) argued in the early 1970s, diversion schemes from criminal justice (including probation, drug treatment centres, halfway houses, employment schemes and so on) act to increase the frequency and intensity of state supervision. This allows an intensification of pains, which are, however, obscured through their bureaucratized functions of reporting and information sharing. Where there was a person who had committed a crime within a context they are now reduced to the information recorded on their file. This dehumanization and intensification of pains has also allowed for the merged prison and probation system to create a totalizing whole system of punishment. Levinas (1969) distinguishes between totalizers and infinitizers, with the former being satisfied with themselves and the systems that they can organize and control and the latter, being dissatisfied, striving for what is other than themselves. In the UK the Kaye and Gibbs (2010) report bemoans an 'existential confusion' at the heart of probation practice, where rehabilitative interventions are placed front and centre of community orders, and not punishment. The report cites the lack of public confidence in community orders and a foreword by Dame Louise Casey (the Victims and Witnesses Commissioner) laments this lack of 'common sense' on the part of the Probation Service and calls for punishment first. The tone and intent of this report are strikingly retributive and at odds with how recipients of community orders view those orders and their punitive intent (see, for example, Andrade et al, 2021).

Interpretive mercy

The beginning of redemption lies outside the sovereignty of the state, with the Kingdom of God calling out retributive justice and populist retributivism. My freedom as a criminal justice practitioner is my humanity, which exists prior to the demands of justice and my professional role. My embracing of forgiveness overcomes my otherness to allow an embodiment of difference that is victim focused, criminal focused and community focused. This change is driven by individual practice even in the most violent situations. To initiate the genuinely new and transformative is to descend into the hell, the mimetic violence experienced in communities and between victims and criminals. Father Alec Reid, through understanding the necessity of descending into the hell of sectarianism, was foundational to the peace process in Northern Ireland from 1983 until the Good Friday Agreement (McKeever, 2017). Father Reid's approach was to listen meticulously to what the conflicting parties were saying about their understanding of the ongoing conflict; he did not judge but listened and encouraged dialogue. As McKeever (2017: 6) describes, Reid was a 'no-man's-land man', as demonstrated by his visits to Liz, a Presbyterian woman who lived on the other sides of the 'peace line' from the Clonard Community where Reid lived. Reid saw himself as a servant of Christ in a situation of political conflict and felt called by the Holy Spirit to reach out and work with people who were 'on the other side'. Following violence that had occurred along the peace line, Reid visited Liz, seeking a reconciliation with someone from the 'other community', and expected an angry reception. She was taken aback to see a Catholic priest at her door but listened to what he had to say and graciously invited him in. On crossing what was for him an alien, even a hostile world ... he realised that he was among friends ... There was a wall hanging placed over the kitchen door ... (which) opened onto the wall of the peace line. Facing out onto the peace line was the message: 'Love one another'. Suddenly there was a bridge instead of a gulf, between the people of that house and himself. It was a bridge of common ideals where he could meet in friendship and love. (McKeever, 2017: 7)

Poiesis and creativity

Through poiesis, opposites can be reconciled in the presence and actions of the criminal justice worker and their multiple readings of the world, their own self-narrative, which they bring to the relationship with the other. In this liminal space, they become a paraclete for the other, with the emerging experience becoming the basis for ongoing narrative that creates practitioner wisdom and role models for others to aspire to. This is foundational to the practitioner's own self-narrative. These myths often originate in the moment, a *sui generis* irruption or event, and thus cannot be prescribed or predicted. However, self-narrative is also foundational to interpreting the law and tradition. In Greek mythology the Titaness Mnemosyne is the communal memory of the tribe and her sister Themis is its communal law and custom, who come into conflict with each other, whereas in the Judeo–Christian tradition,

> Mercy and truth have met,
> Righteousness and peace will kiss. (Psalm 85: 11)

Further, the Muses (the source of artistic and philosophical creativity) are the daughters of memory. The English poet John Heath-Stubbs (1977: 16) argues that '[m]yth in its original sense of a sacred story is not something constructed but given ... Because myth is a means of exploring human potentiality, the poet must revalue experience and become a revolutionary ... traditionally the poet is the retailer of myths.' Likewise, Peter Levi (1977: 100) states: 'Poetry is some kind of human reasoning, and however multiple its reading of the world may be it comes from the spring of all reasoning, even outside poetry. It has to be truthful within the possible limits of language we all talk.'

The Eucharist (Gr: *eukharistia*, 'thanksgiving', from Gr: *eukharistos* 'grateful', *eu*, 'well' and *kharizesthai*, 'offer graciously' (from *kharis* 'grace') also known as the Lord's Supper and Communion) is central to most Christian Churches' liturgical life. The celebration of the Eucharist is based upon Jesus' celebration of the Jewish feast of Passover (both a remembrance and celebration for the Jewish people of God delivering them from captivity in Egypt) with his followers before he was executed (the last meals of condemned prisoners in the US are still a source of fascination (see Rayner, 2020)).

> Then he took bread, and when he had given thanks, he broke it and gave it to them saying 'This is my body given for you; do this in remembrance of me.' He did the same with the cup after supper, and said, 'This cup is the new covenant in my blood poured out for you.' (Luke 22: 19–20)

Interpretation of this text has been a source of controversy down the ages, with Catholic and Orthodox traditions accepting the consecrated bread and wine as the body and blood of Christ, and the Protestant traditions seeing it as symbolic representation of the body and blood of Christ. A key focus for debate was to explain how it was possible for the bread and wine to become the body and blood of Christ and what this might actually mean. In the Catholic and Orthodox traditions, when the bread and wine is offered up in the Mass, and the priest says the words of consecration, a process of transubstantiation takes place and Christ becomes substantially present in the bread and wine. Aquinas explained this through Aristotle's distinction between a thing's substance and accidents: the substance of the bread and wine is now the body of Christ, while the accidents of bread and wine remain (its appearance and flavour). On first appearance, what may seem an arcane and fruitless, scholastic (angels dancing on pinheads) argument actually presents us with a model of being for the other and a source of self within criminal justice practice. Hemming (2000: 180) discusses the reappearance of this concept in philosophical discourse in relation to the work of Judith Butler and Slavoj Žižek:

> Transubstantiation here names the point at which something comes to be seen for what it really is, *despite appearances* ... (and) is itself a replacement for the Newtonian cosmos, and in a forceful confrontation with it. For both Butler and Žižek, transubstantiation represents a certain 'being taken into the know': What Aquinas would have understood by 'intellection[2]', but now devoid of God. Transubstantiation is for them a 'point at which' something which can be taken for one thing is in fact known to be another, *but still could be taken for what it was taken for at first.* (emphases in the original)

We can explore this further through the phenomenology of Merleau-Ponty, wherein we find a revitalization of theological and sacramental ideas in a post-metaphysical language (Kearney, 2010). A Eucharistic presence and the meeting of the other, even within the limits of language, is itself a cause for celebration, a jouissance of the moment, the potential to inaugurate and actualize new life. Through an act of continual giving, the Eucharist returns us to what is real rather than metaphysical – the body, flesh, blood – and is an immanent irruption into our chronological life, thus presenting sparks of possibility and a reassembling of energies for the other. These Eucharistic moments, while not always easy to discern, can occur even in the highly prescriptive routines of modern criminal justice. If the analogy for the treadmill of justice is that of Sisyphus, condemned to a continual pushing of a boulder up a hill, then we might agree with Camus (1998) that Sisyphus experiences a moment of freedom just as he puts his shoulder to the boulder. This may not be much to go on, but these ruptures glimpsing the human occur frequently, revealing both the absurdity of our situations (Camus, 1988) but also the possibility of the gift and secular epiphanies. In Eucharistic terms, the meal, the sharing of a cup of tea, meeting service users in McDonalds, sharing a joke, becomes the opening, the place of dialogue (see Pycroft et al, 2015 for examples of creative practice with 'high risk and dangerous' adolescents) where causality is suspended and people are revealed as they are in themselves.

As an act of anamnesis, there is a remembrance of wrongs committed, but the celebration is a new future actualized through the creative rather than retentive use of memory. Bergson (see Notopolous, 1938) makes this distinction between memory that imagines and a memory that repeats and is implicit within a hermeneutical phenomenology of the Eucharist. The bureaucratic within criminal justice is the memory that repeats, whereas 'the creative use of memory ... is *movement* of thought' (Notopolous, 1938: 482, emphasis in the original). Notopolous discusses the oral tradition of Greek literature and demonstrates how the written word impacts on creativity and how the book can become a lifeless thing. The word may be a stepping stone, but knowledge and creative apprehension are fundamental. Reading the file on the criminal may be the first principle of risk management and public protection (Dr Dennis Gough, private correspondence) but only the oral mind engaging with the reality of the other can glimpse and memorize what is possible, even incredible. The 'almost but not quite' cannot be grasped and reduced to writing.

A paradigm of therapeutic immanence (expressed by Bergson (1988) as each moment as individual film frames) requires the development of a coherent narrative for both the worker and the service user. In the creation of this narrative, the practitioner becomes an animate and active giver rather than carrying out impersonal duty. This profanation of the sacrament (Yoder, 2020) and a rejection of metaphysics, to embody the real and to embody the difference, requires a vocation (literally a call, summons, invitation) for embeddedness (embodiment) in the structures of justice.

Conclusion

You know how it is. You go to write something, a letter, an essay, an article, a book, or you start working with a new and challenging service user. In your mind, you are clear what you are doing, you are excited having glimpsed the possibilities to do good work. Waking up of a morning your crepuscular semi-conscious state has made wonderful connections, you glimpse 'the thing in itself' its haecceity, you are up for the challenge. You go to work, make that cup of coffee, sit down with a blank piece of paper or computer screen, talk to colleagues, meet the service users, but then it's gone! You seem to be dragged in by the complexity of the challenges, with the connections not quite so vivid or obvious – the *enargeia* is dissipated. Why is this? In part because the reductionist and calculating mind, in needing to try to make sense of the intuition, its content, presentation and acceptability to others, loses the whole picture. This is not helped by working in bureaucratized neoliberal institutions (including universities), where your work is shaped and performance managed, subjected to endless reviews, the demands of file keeping, and supervision. The risk is that despite the importance of the work and our own motivation, as with *Brideshead Revisited* and Charles Ryder's sojourn with the army, we are stripped of all enchantment (Waugh, 1964).

In the work of enchantment there is no conclusion, only the ongoing work of self to be more open to the other through apprehending what is real, discerning the traces of metaphysical violence and responding with the gift of love. Central to our argument is that modern theological and philosophical resources allow both a rereading of the Judaeo-Christian contribution to the development of ideas of justice, punishment and their consequences, and also what it means to be an authentic practitioner through learning to see. Within these resources we find rich seams of dialogue between different perspectives that allow us to develop a peacemaking perspective in criminal justice based on being-for-others. We are not evangelical about our criminological position but are simply providing a point of orientation and departure. The *logos* (spirit) of our argument is always in the hermeneutical space between victims, offenders and communities. Thus, our exploration and explanation are also between humanities and science, cultural and critical criminology, criminology and victimology (and so on). As Frantz Fanon (2021) so powerfully argues, language is but one, though nonetheless essential, dimension in our being-for-others. Without language we cannot communicate and if we cannot communicate then I am not able to understand that which you need from me or me from you. Empathy and intuition require a language that can convey the richness of an encounter (in phenomenology the content of the phenomena can never be exhausted), that overcomes reductionism and decontextualization, and in no way do we underestimate the difficulties of communication. Our narrative has been a lifetime's work and in communicating it we accept that some of the concepts discussed in this book are challenging and take some working through. We have kept the advice of Jacques Derrida in mind: 'One shouldn't complicate things for the pleasure of complicating, but one should also never simplify or pretend to be sure of such simplicity where there is none. If things were simple, word would have gotten round ...' (Derrida, 1988: 119).

We have tried to articulate an approach and language predicated on a revelation of truth as dynamic, creative and loving. Science itself reveals the dynamism and endless creativity of the universe and contexts in which we live. We are not separate from, but in the systems that we live and study. Theology and myth reveal love, and through that love a reinforcement of dynamism and creativity. This creativity reveals the limits of reductionism and fragmentation both in thought, method and the practices of justice. The separation of mind, matter and time in trying to establish causal relationships not only prevents us from understanding the whole, but also becomes a basis for moral judgement grounded in ontotheology (we create gods in our own violent image).

In human relationships forgiveness opens a space of possibility and so is the beginning of the process and not the end, and is the place of embrace rather than judgement and the othering of difference. The language that emerges in hermeneutical space cannot be apprehended or articulated by reductionist thinking. Reductionism is either/or, with the utilitarian solution being a conflation of punishment and rehabilitation, the outcome of which is increasingly harsh penal measures and high reoffending rates, resulting in a perpetuation of harms to all. Critical criminology in the genealogy of de Sade, Nietzsche, Heidegger and Foucault provides no solution to violence and may both exacerbate it and increasingly lead to a breakdown in coherent thought structure. The Marxist tradition, in itself a demythologization of Judaeo-Christianity, assumes a dialectical resolution and so denies individual experience and history in building an idealized future.

Given the utilitarian hegemony in ethics and political economy and the self-evidently poor outcomes for all from the processes of justice, the question becomes what is going on here, why is nothing changing? We have used Girard's analysis of mimetic behaviour as a heuristic for understanding the relationships between the sacred and sacrificial in the practices of justice. In particular we have argued that what masquerades as rationality serves to conceal the scapegoat mechanism and that the Judaeo-Christian tradition reveals and calls out the functions that justice serves in establishing 'social cohesion'. The revolving door of justice that punishes individuals on the margins of society is a conveyor belt of sacrifice that is processed by organizations based on impersonal office rather than the personal and redemptive qualities. This dominance of the impersonal becomes evident in rehabilitation, with the argument still persisting that adherence to the model of RNR is what determines success from interventions (for example Vincent et al, 2021). This becomes a fundamentalism and teleology, arguing that at the future point at which organizations conform exactly to the requirements of the model then everything will be perfect. At this point, of course, human practitioners become redundant and can be replaced by algorithm-driven automata.

Rather than more of the impersonal and mechanistic the practitioner becomes authentic through a discovery and affirmation of their subjectivity. It is at the level of the individual practitioner that we have chosen to focus because it is at this level that real change can happen. The institutional and social context is important and this will form the basis of further scholarship on our part but we have wanted to challenge the problem of the relationship between conformity and creativity for practitioners. As Charles Taylor (1989) would say, we have attempted to identify sources of ourselves and to provide an account of those selves to the reader in the hope that this example of a hermeneutical narrative might encourage others to do the same.

The 'Will to meaning' (Frankl, 2014: 20) is a key feature of training in the therapeutic traditions and also social work, where an ongoing commitment to relationship bases our actions on the understanding of our own ongoing complicity in violence. This has been eschewed by criminal justice institutions, whose enshrining of scapegoating mechanisms leads to a totalizing conformity over and above relational creativity. Increasingly legislation for human rights, equality and discrimination is in place, but within these processes are areas that involve decision making based on judgement. The discretion of practitioners and managers is fraught with difficulty and partly explains the emphasis on institutional conformity and algorithm-based judgement tools (see Jennings and Pycroft, 2012). However, algorithms simply reflect inbuilt bias and racism (see Arrigo and Sellers, 2021) whereas people best respond to what is authentically human, that is the key message from myth, religion and psychoanalysis.

Within criminal justice organizations the capacity for individual practitioners to be authentically human and not overwhelmed by routinization and bureaucracy, which drain energy from the human encounter, is a challenge. This is not to deny the hard work and good intentions of individual practitioners and organizations and the examples of good practice that exist, but is a recognition of the totalizing impact of the justice system which is subservient to political economy. To a large degree the organization of individual and collective resistance will be determined by institutional memory. Normally historical path dependence argues that the past constrains the future; what institutions remember frames their tasks, and that amnesia is a barrier to organizational learning (Corbett et al, 2017). This actually presents an interesting paradox for probation services in the UK and US as its theological origins have been institutionalized. Theology is of course also institutionalized in the system of punishment but we find divergent theologies (Burke, 2021), with the former as a rationale for working with and helping disadvantaged criminals still a driver for people becoming probation officers. There are also grounds for hope with, for example, Lee et al (2021), who, in a survey of millennials' attitudes to corrections in the US, found the majority in favour of redemptive and inclusionary policies. We move forward by speaking truth, remembering the past, honouring victims and their traumas but enabling criminals to be genuinely redeemed through inclusion rather than exclusion. This is not about denying the past, or not honouring victims, it is about peacebuilding and breaking cycles of violence that emerge in everyday lives.

The culture of the sacred sacrificial is as ancient as humanity and will not be let go of easily, whatever alternative vision comes along. The necessity for scapegoats can be compelling and overpowering for all of us. But as James Baldwin (Peck, 2016) says in relation to being a black man in America, '[w]hat white people have to do, is try and find out in their own hearts why it was necessary to have a n****r in the first place, because I'm not a n****r, I'm a man, but if you think I'm a n****r, it means you need it'. The need for scapegoats has increased in an increasingly uncertain and globalized world, and in both the UK and US there has been a resurgence of the politics of sacrifice driving populism. The violence of those politics demonstrates why there can be no conservative restoration of what has gone before or a new future created through using the innocence of victims to justify the creation of more victims. This is Satan casting out Satan (see Chapter 4). Again James Baldwin (Peck, 2016) argues, '[n]ot everything that is faced can be changed. But nothing can be changed until it has been faced. History is not the past. It is the present. We carry our history with us. We are our history. If we pretend otherwise, we literally are criminals.'

In the current political contexts, the chances of facing the reality of criminal justice systems, which themselves are criminal in many of their actions, is highly unlikely and explains why no mainstream political party is advocating for penal reform despite the obvious failures. It is this mobilization of violence that is at the heart of 'community justice', where community remains an idealized notion, taken for granted, under-examined and least articulated. The potential for violence at the heart of community is used to garner support (see Gorringe, 2002) and we start to catch glimpses of this when we understand the ease with which communities can be mobilized for restrictive measures, for example community notification or exclusion in crime prevention and public protection. The community, normally, is not mobilized in the same way to support constructive efforts at rehabilitation for offenders. There are examples of community-based restorative programmes such as Circles of Support and Accountability (for a discussion in relation to the theology of atonement see Gorringe, 2021). Restorative justice is often seen as synonymous with community justice (McEvoy and Mica, 2002) but any reconciliation between the victim and the offender (which may or may not involve forgiveness) has no impact on the wider community or any real connection with it. In fact, debates about forgiveness and its relationship to justice are as contested in restorative justice as elsewhere (see Armour and Umbreit, 2005).

Maybe the character of Joseph Grand in Camus' *The Plague* (2002) best signifies our anxiety about what to do. He is not only trying to write to his estranged wife and cannot find the words, but he also wants to write the perfect book, but cannot get past the first line despite his copious notes and preparation. Neoliberal practices and organizational regression to the mean (see Jennings, 2014) have no interest in getting beyond the first line, only to the bottom line of finance and budgets. In fact, there is a terror in the face of the creativity that would bring so much humanity and thus success to the practices of justice. That creativity is in part the responsibility of the individual practitioner, and their own authenticity, who needs to challenge their own organizational contexts to bring the radically new (see Pycroft, 2019).

Working in the modern neoliberal university life is very similar in many ways to working in the deadening bureaucracy of the criminal justice system. The question becomes how to get past the first line and to find and develop a creative space where possibilities can be actualized. For us this is essential as an increasingly administrative criminology that is data- and model driven does not allow for an engagement with the very conditions (context) that enable a process of redemption. The qualities of the practitioner are central to this process (see, for example, Miller and Rollnick, 2002 for a summary of the literature) but it is those very qualities that are eroded and sidelined in contemporary practice.

It is the hard-won qualities of the practitioner and the demonstration of authenticity that open up the space of possibility where new realities can be engaged with. The opportunities may be few and far between but nonetheless emerge in the course of practice. These spaces have been variously described as 'rock bottom' or the 'teachable moment' or 'hesed' or 'phase space' but where there is a confluence of the dynamics of structure, agency and time. It is only through understanding our conjunction in that space with the other that we can realize (actualize) our own potential as practitioners. For us redemption is not a conservative restoration (there are no golden ages) but an actualization of the real that has the potential to transvaluate and transubstantiate interpersonal justice, mediated by the practitioner and their jouissance in embracing the other.

This can only happen if we have the courage to be (Tillich, 1971) through seeking to identify those that we ourselves are scapegoating and the rivalries that have led to their creation. In this respect we both agree that our best learning about ourselves has been from examining our relationships with the people that we find most difficult. Engaging with and reflecting on these difficulties tells us something about the projection of our own shadow, our complicity in violence and our hearts turned in on themselves. It requires other people that we trust, good therapeutic supervision in a community of practitioners that enable us to engage in this difficult work.

This is not wishful thinking or naivety and is between the existential and the humanistic in engaging with both limitations and possibilities, mediated by the practitioner and their mobilization of resources. It is not necessarily an argument against complete decarceration and we have both worked with dangerous individuals who should not be released into the community for the protection of others and themselves. It is an argument for accepting people as they are, prior to any judgement or requirements for justice. It is only in accepting this humanity, the humanity that is revealed in God becoming human, that we can embrace our responsibility to victims, offenders and communities. This anthropic responsibility is a gift of grace each to the other, the realities and potential of which are revealed in a range of myths, stories and experiences that should no longer be ignored or denigrated, and whose non-religious interpretation may provide an important missing link between criminology, victimology, and the knowledge and skills necessary for criminal justice practice.

Notes

Chapter 1

[1] https://voegelinview.com/a-night-in-heidelberg-pt-1/

[2] For biographical details see Kelley (2005) and Looney (2015).

Chapter 2

[1] The scholastics were rooted in the dogma of their religious traditions but sought to use Ancient Greek philosophical thought to further their arguments in relation to society.

[2] In an interesting article Pauling (2021) discusses how immanentizing the eschaton is a problem for apocalyptic politics on both the Left and Right. The argument against has been a mantra of the Right since the 1960s, but the attack on Capitol Hill on 6 January 2021 was replete with eschatological language conflating Donald Trump with Jesus Christ. The inaugurated eschatology is not based on a will to power through particular forms of politics or policies, rather it is the ability to speak truth, which can only be truth if it is not predicated upon the demonization of the other.

[3] Kant considers God to be the unconditioned principle that is necessary for the moral life to exist through practical reason. His thinking contains both a concept of natural law and social contract as a consequence of that law. Natural law as an expression of divine law had been articulated by the medieval scholastics in Christianity, Islam and Judaism, but Kantian thought forms the basis for a philosophical rather than theological interpretation.

Chapter 3

[1] A feminine designation of God other than in relation to the Holy Spirit (see page 108) appears in neither Protestant nor Catholic theology, however in following Marion's argument of a god beyond designation it is appropriately consistent to use this language of radical equality.

Chapter 5

[1] Storytelling in criminal justice and situations of conflict is used extensively by the Forgiveness Project https://www.theforgivenessproject.com/

[2] It is interesting that the tradition of pardoning criminals has continued as a presidential power in the US, despite the constitutional separation of state and religion, whereas in the UK, with a constitutional monarchy where the monarch is the head of the established Church of England, the last royal pardons were granted in 1897. This was during the Diamond Jubilee of Queen Victoria and they were used to political advantage in ruling India by releasing nearly 20,000 prisoners.

[3] Saul and Paul are the same person, but St Paul or Paul is the usual designation. We use the names interchangeably.

[4] There is dispute about which of the 13 epistles can be attributed to Paul. Modern scholarship attributes seven (see Ehrman, 2018).

Chapter 6

[1] See Chapter 2.

[2] The terms 'alcoholic' or 'alcoholism' have no clinical validity, despite being commonly used, including by practitioners. The World Health Organization replaced these concepts

in 1977 with Dependence Syndromes, now the basis for medical and psychiatric classification in the form of DSM-5 and ICD-10.

Chapter 7

[1] Merleau-Ponty (1968) argues against reductionism into separate entities of mind and body, subject and so on, as these pairs are also associated and interdependent with each other. This intertwining is a chiasm (*chi* is the 22nd letter of the Greek alphabet (X)), a crossing over combining both subjective experience and objective existence in the body (as flesh – *chair*. See Chapter 5). As Voss (2013) argues, the radical nature of Merleau-Ponty's philosophy is the emphasis on relationality, ambiguity and our embeddedness in the world and our connection with the other.

[2] Hemming (2000: 173) explains that 'transubstantiation enacts intellection: In undertaking a certain to-be-known, it requires that intellection itself is the way in which the Redemption in Christ is known *to be*. The real transubstantiation is enacted in the intellect of the believer, yet not in consequence of his or her will, but entirely in consequence of God's power' (emphasis in the original).

References

Abdel Haleem, M (2016) *The Qur'an*. Oxford. Oxford University Press

Agamben, G (2011) *The Kingdom and the Glory: For a Theological Genealogy of Economy and Government*. Stanford. Stanford University Press

Alison, J (2003) *On Being Liked*. Norwich. Darton, Longman and Todd

Alison, J (2019) 'The Unexpected Shape of Forgiveness', http://jamesalison.com/the-unexpected-shape-of-forgiveness/

Allan, A (2008) 'Functional Apologies in Law', *Psychiatry, Psychology and Law* 15(3): 369–81

Améry, J (1999) *At the Mind's Limits*. London. Granta

Andrade, J, Cruz, A and Cunha, O (2021) 'Community Sanctions: Offenders' Perceptions About Their Appropriateness', *European Journal of Probation* https://doi.org/10.1177/20662203211014161

Arendt, H (1961) *Between Past and Future: Eight Exercises in Political Thought*. New York. Viking

Arendt, H (2006) *Eichmann in Jerusalem: A Report on the Banality of Evil*. London. Penguin Classics

Armour, M and Umbreit, M (2005) 'The Paradox of Forgiveness in Restorative Justice' in E Worthington (ed) *Handbook of Forgiveness*. Hove. Routledge. 49–503

Armstrong, K (2015) *St Paul: The Misunderstood Apostle*. London. Atlantic Books

Arrigo, B and Seller, B (eds) (2021) *The Pre-Crime Society: Crime, Culture and Control in the Ultramodern Age*. Bristol. Bristol University Press

Ashley, J (2015) *Interruptions: Mysticism, Politics and Theology in the Work of Johann Baptist Metz*. Notre Dame. University of Notre Dame Press

Aulen, G. (2003) *Christus Victor: An Historical Study of the Three Main Types of the Idea of Atonement*. Oregon. Wipf & Stock Publishers

Augustine, St. (1958) *City of God*. London. Penguin Books

Bachelard, G (1969) *The Poetics of Reverie*. Boston. Beacon Press Books

Badiou, A (2003) *Saint Paul: The Foundation of Universalism*. Stanford. Stanford University Press

Baker, J and Whitehead, A (2020) 'God's penology: Belief in a masculine God predicts support for harsh criminal punishment and militarism', *Punishment and Society* 22(2): 135–60

Barclay, J (2015) *Paul & the Gift*. Grand Rapids. Eerdmans

Barker, M (2004) *The Great High Priest: The Temple Roots of Christian Liturgy*. London. T&T Clark

Barnes, J (ed) (1995) 'The Nicomachean Ethics' in *The Complete Works of Aristotle. The Revised Oxford Tanslation: Volume One*. Chichester. Princeton University Press. 1729–867

Bartollas, C (1985) *Correctional Treatment: Theory and Practice*. Englewood Cliffs. Prentice-Hall

Bartollas, C (2019) *From Disgrace to Dignity: Redemption in the Life of Willie Rico Johnson*. Eugene Oregon: Cascade Books

Bartollas, C., Schmalleger, F. and Turner, M (2019) *Juvenile Delinquency (10th ed)* Hudson Street: Pearson

Bash, A (2015) *Forgiveness: A Theology*. Eugene. Cascade Books

Bergson, H (1988) *Matter and Memory* (trans N Paul and W Palmer). New York. Zone Books

Bergson, H (1999) *Metaphysics: An Introduction*. London. Hackett Publishing

Bethge, E (2000) *Dietrich Bonhoeffer: A Biography*. Minneapolis. Augsburg Fortress

Bettelheim, B (1960) *The Informed Heart*. London. Penguin Books

Bohm, D (1980) *Wholeness and the Implicate Order*. London. Routledge

Bohm, D. (1990) 'A New Theory of the Relationship of Mind and Matter', *Philosophical Psychology* 3(2): 1–14

Bohm, D. and Hiley, B. (1987) 'An Ontological Basis for the Quantum Theory', *Physics Reports* 144: 323–48

Bracken, C (2018) 'The Deaths of Moses: The Death Penalty and the Division of Sovereignty', *Critical Research on Religion* 6(2): 168–183

Braithwaite, J (2016) 'Redeeming the 'F' Word in Restorative Justice', *Oxford Journal of Law and Religion* 5: 79–93

Breton, S (1988) *A Radical Philosophy of Saint Paul*. New York. Columbia University Press

Buber, M (2013) *I and Thou*. London. Bloomsbury Academic

Burke, K (1954) *Permanence and Change: An Anatomy of Purpose*. Berkeley. University of California Press

Burke, L (2021) 'The Quality of Mercy in Probation Practice' in A Millie (ed) *Criminology and Public Theology: On Hope, Mercy and Restoration*. Bristol. Bristol University Press. 195–216

Camus, A (1988) *The Myth of Sisyphus*. London. Penguin Books

Camus, A (1989) *The Stranger*. London. Vintage Books

Camus, A (2000) *The Rebel*. London. Penguin Books

Camus, A (2002) *The Plague*. London. Penguin Books

Carlen, P (2013) 'Penal Imaginaries: Against Rehabilitation; For Reparative Justice' in K Carrington, M. Ball, O'Brien and J. Tauri (eds) *Crime, Justice and Social Democracy*. London. Palgrave.

Cash, J (2004) *Presents a Concert Behind Prison Walls*. DVD. Eagle Eye Media

Chapman, G (2014) *Catechism of the Catholic Church*. London. Bloomsbury

Christie, N (1977) 'Conflicts as Property', *British Journal of Criminology* 17(1): 1–15

Cilliers, P (2005) 'Complexity, Deconstruction and Relativism', *Theory, Culture, Society* 22(5): 255–67

Clements, K (2000) 'Book Review of "Act and Being: Transcendental Philosophy and Ontology in Systematic Theology" by Dietrich Bonhoeffer', *Scottish Journal of Theology* 53(2): 245–58

Cohen, S (2016) 'Aristotle's Metaphysics' in Stanford Encyclopedia of Philosophy https://plato.stanford.edu/entries/aristotle-metaphysics

Cone, J (2017) *The Cross and the Lynching Tree*. Maryknoll. Orbis Books

Corbett, J, Grube, D, Lovell, H and Scott, R (2017) 'Singular Memory or Institutional Memories? Toward a Dynamic Approach', *Governance* 31: 555–73

Cotkin, G (2005) *Existential America*. New York. Johns Hopkins University Press

Cover, R (1995) 'Violence and the Word' in Minow, M, Ryan, M and Sarat, A (eds) (1995) *Narrative, Violence and the Law: The Essays of Robert Cover*. Michigan. Michigan University Press. 203–38

Crewe, D. (2019) 'Blame, Responsibility and Peacemaking', *Journal of Theoretical and Philosophical Criminology* 11(1): 1–17

Critchley, S (1997) 'What Is Continental Philosophy', *International Journal of Philosophical Studies* 5(3): 347–65

Davis, C (ed) (2009) *The Monstrosity of Christ: Paradox or Dialectic*. Cambridge, MA. Massachusetts Institute of Technology Press

Davis, Z and Steinbock, A (2018) 'Max Scheler', https://plato.stanford.edu/entries/scheler/

Derbyshire, J (2013) 'Heidegger in France: Nazism and Philosophy', *The Guardian*, 13 December

Derrida, J (1988) *Limited Inc*. Evanston. Northwestern University Press

Derrida, J (2002) *On Cosmopolitanism and Forgiveness*. London. Routledge

Dodds, C (1980) *The Parables of the Kingdom*. Glasgow. William Collins & Sons

Dumouchel, P (2011) 'De la Méconnaissance', *Lebenswelt* 1: 97–111

Dupuy, JP (2013) *The Mark of the Sacred*. Stanford. Stanford University Press

Dykes, L (2001) 'Non-violent "Religion": The Community of Scapegoats', *Contagion: Journal of Violence, Mimesis and Culture* 8(1): 90–113

Eddy, J and Beilby, P (2006) 'The Atonement: An Introduction' in P Beilby and J Eddy (eds) *The Nature of Atonement: Four Views*. Illinois. IVP Academic. 9–21

Ehrman, B (2018) *The Triumph of Christianity: How a Forbidden Religion Swept the World*. St Ives. One World Publications

Estes, D. (2008) *The Temporal Mechanics of the Fourth Gospel: A Theory of Hermeneutical Relativity in the Gospel of John*. Boston. Brill

Eubank, N (2010) 'A Disconcerting Prayer: On the Originality of Luke 23:34a', *Journal of Biblical Literature* 129(3): 521–36

Fanon, F (2021) *Black Skin, White Masks*. London. Penguin

Falque, E (2015) 'This Is My Body: Contribution to a Philosophy of the Eucharist' in R Kearney and B Treanor (eds) *Carnal Hermeneutics*. New York. Fordham University Press. 279–94

Fiddes, P. (2016) 'Restorative Justice and the Theological Dynamic of Forgiveness', *Oxford Journal of Law and Religion* 5: 54–65

Foucault, M (1977) *Discipline and Punish: The Birth of the Prison*. London. Allen Lane

Francis (2015) 'Letter to the President of the International Commission against the Death Penalty' *L'Osservatore Romano*, 7

Frankl, V (2014) *The Will to Meaning*. Hungerford. Plume

Freud, S (2001) *The Future of an Illusion, Civilization and its Discontents and Other Works. The Standard Edition of the Complete Psychological Works of Sigmund Freud, Volume XXI (1927–31)*. London. Vintage Books

Fujimura, M (2020) *A Theology of Making: Art + Faith*. London. Yale University Press

Gålnander, R (2019) 'Desistance from Crime–to What? Exploring Future Aspirations and Their Implications for Processes of Desistance', *Feminist Criminology* DOI: 10.1177/1557085119879236

Ganiel, G and Yohanis, J (2019) *Considering Grace: Presbyterians and the Troubles*. Newbridge. Merrion Press

Gibbs, R (2006) 'Verdict and Sentence: Cover and Levinas on the Robe of Justice', *The Journal of Jewish Thought and Philosophy* 14(1–2): 73–89

Girard, R (1978) *Things Hidden Since the Foundation of the World*. London. Continuum

Girard, R (2001) *I see Satan Fall like Lightening*. Leominster. Gracewing

Girard, R (2007) *Evolution and Conversion: Dialogues on the Origins of Culture*. London. Continuum

Girard, R (2014) *The One by Whom Scandal Comes*. East Lansing. Michigan University Press

Glatt, E (2013) 'The Unanimous Verdict According to the Talmud: Ancient Law Providing Insight into Modern Legal Theory', *Pace International Law Review Online Companion* 3(10): 316–35

Goldman, L and Thompson, P (2019) *Avicenna and the Aristotelian Left*. New York. Columbia University Press

Gorringe, T (1996) *God's Just Vengeance*. Cambridge. Cambridge University Press

Gorringe, T (2002) 'The Prisoner as Scapegoat: Some Skeptical Remarks on Present Penal Policy' in T O'Connor and N Pallone (eds) *Religion, the Community and the Rehabilitation of Criminal Offenders*. London. Haworth Press. 249–57

Gorringe, T (2021) 'Interpreting the Cross: Religion, Structures of Feeling, and Penal Theory and Practice' in A Millie (ed) *Criminology and Public Theology: On Hope, Mercy and Restoration*. Bristol. Bristol University Press. 93–110

Grau, M (2004) *Of Divine Economy: Refinancing Redemption*. New York. T and T Clarke

Green, R (1969) 'Ernst Bloch's Revision of Atheism', *The Journal of Religion* 49(2): 128–35

Grieve, J (2014) 'The Stephen Lawrence Inquiry: A case study in policing and complexity' in A. Pycroft and C. Bartollas (eds) *Applying Complexity Theory: Whole Systems Approaches to Criminal Justice and Social Work*. Bristol. Policy Press. 141–58

Griswold, C. (2007) *Forgiveness: A Philosophical Exploration*. Cambridge. Cambridge University Press

Guardini, R (2013) *The End of the Modern World*. Wilmington. ISI Books

Haltemann, M (1998) 'Onto Theology' in *Routledge Encyclopaedia of Philosophy*, DOI: 0.4324/9780415249126-K115-1

Hanson, A and Hanson, R (1985) *Reasonable Belief: A Survey of the Christian Faith*. Oxford. Oxford University Press

Harill, J (2002) 'Coming of Age and Putting on Christ: The Toga Virilis Ceremony, Its Paraenesis, and Paul's Interpretation of Baptism in Galatians', *Novum Testamentum* 44(3): 252–77

Hathaway, O (2003) 'Path Dependence in the Law: The Course and Pattern of Legal Change in a Common Law System' *John M. Olin Centre for Studies in Law, Economics, and Public Policy Working Papers*. Yale Law School

Haven, C (2018). *Evolution of Desire: A Life of René Girard*. East Lansing. Michigan University Press

Hayden, C and Gough, D (2010) *Implementing Restorative Justice in Children's Residential Care*. Bristol. Policy Press

Heath-Stubbs, J (1977) 'Myth and Poetry', *Agenda: Special Issue on Myth* 15(2–3): 16–17

Heidegger, M (1978) *Being and Time*. Oxford. Blackwell

Hemming, L (2000) 'After Heidegger: Transubstantiation', *Heythrop Journal* XLI: 170–86

Hodder, I (2012) *Entangled: An Archaeology of the Relationships between Humans and Things*. Chichester. Wiley-Blackwell

Hodges, M (2008) 'Re-thinking Time's Arrow: Bergson, Deleuze and the Anthropology of Time', *Anthropological Theory* 8(4): 399–429

Hoekema, A (2000) 'The "Christology" of the Japanese Novelist Shusaku Endo', *Exchange* 29(3): 230–48

Holder, H (1999) *Alcohol and the Community: A Systems Approach to Prevention*. Cambridge. Cambridge University Press

Hunter, B and Farrall, S (2018) 'Emotions, Future Selves and the Process of Desistance', *British Journal of Criminology* 58: 291–398

Inwood, M (2016) 'Book Review of Wittgenstein and Heidegger edited by D. Egan, S. Reynolds and A. Wendland', *The Philosophical Quarterly* 66(265): 867–69

Ishoy, A and Kruis (2019) 'A Peacemaking Approach to Desistance from Crime', *Critical Criminology* 27(2): 211–27

Israel, H (1998) 'The Nazi Origins of Eduard Pernkopf's Topographische Anatomie des Menschen', *The Reference Librarian* 29(61–62): 131–46

Jankélévitch, V (2005) *Forgiveness*. Chicago. University of Chicago Press

Jennings, P (2014) 'Risk, Attractors and Organisational Behaviour' in A. Pycroft and C. Bartollas (eds) *Applying Complexity Theory: Whole Systems Approaches to Criminal Justice and Social Work*. Bristol. Policy Press. 39–58

Jennings, P and Pycroft, A (2012) 'The Numbers Game: A Systems Perspective on Risk' in A Pycroft and S Clift (eds) *Risk and Rehabilitation: The Treatment and Management of Substance Misuse and Mental Health Problems in the Criminal Justice System*. Bristol. Policy Press. 7–20

Jewish Encyclopedia, IX, 514–15, article 'Paraclete' https://www.jewishencyclopedia.com/

Johnston, A (2018) Jaques Lacan, https://plato.stanford.edu/entries/lacan/#OthOedComSex

Jun, N (2007) 'Toward a Girardian Politics', https://www.researchgate.net/publication/252934438_Toward_a_Girardian_Politics

Kasza, J (2016) *Hermeneutics of Evil in the Works of Endō Shūsaku: Between Reading and Writing*. Berne. Peter Lang

Kaye, R and Gibbs, B (2010) *Fitting the Crime: Reforming Community Sentences, Mending the Weak Link in the Sentence Plan*. London. Policy Exchange, https://policyexchange.org.uk/wp-content/uploads/2016/09/fitting-the-crime-nov-10.pdf

Kearney, R (1986) 'Religion and Ideology: Paul Ricoeur's Hermeneutic Conflict', *The Irish Theological Quarterly* 52: 109–26

Kearney, R (1999). 'Aliens and others: Between Girard and Derrida', *Cultural Values* 3(3): 251–62

Kearney, R (2010) *Anatheism (Returning to God after God)*. New York. Columbia University Press

Kearney, R and Zimmerman, J (eds) (2016) *Reimagining the Sacred: Richard Kearney Debates God*. New York. Columbia University Press

Keddie, A (2019) *Class and Power in Roman Palestine: The Socioeconomic Setting of Judaism and Christian Origins*. Cambridge. Cambridge University Press

Kelley, A (2005) 'Translator's Introduction' in V Jankélévitch, *Forgiveness*. Chicago. University of Chicago Press. vii–xxvii

Kitamori, K (1966) *Theology of the Pain of God*. London. SCM Press

Kristeva, J (1989) *Black Sun: Depression and Melancholia*. New York. Columbia University Press

Kristeva, J (2016) 'New Humanism and the Need to Believe: Dialogue with Julia Kristeva' in R Kearney and J Zimmerman (eds) *Reimagining the Sacred*. New York. Columbia University Press. 93–127

Kynes, W (2010) 'God's Grace in the Old Testament: Considering the *Hesed* of the Lord', *Knowing & Doing*, Summer edition: 1–3

Lacan, J (2019) *Desire and Its Interpretation: The Seminar of Jacques Lacan/Book VI*. Cambridge. Polity

Lane, R and Price, A (2005) *Distinctive Catholic Schools, the Formation of Wholeness: Part One, the Reconciliation of Belief and Practice*. Unpublished paper.

Lee, H, Cullen, F, Burton, A and Burton, V (2021) 'Millennials as the Future of Corrections: A Generational Analysis of Public Policy Opinions', *Crime and Delinquency on line first*, https://doi.org/10.1177/00111287211022610

Lenehan, K (2010) 'Symmetries of the Kingdom: Suggestions from Girard and Bonhoeffer on Thinking the Church–State Relation', *Heythrop Journal* 51(4): 567–81

Levi, P (1977) 'Notes on Myth', *Agenda: Special Issue on Myth* 15(2–3): 97–100

Levi, P (1985) *The Periodic Table*. Bungay. Abacus Books

Levinas, E (1969) *Totality and Infinity: An Essay on Exteriority*. Pittsburgh. Duquesne University Press

Liu, J (2017) 'The New Asian Paradigm: A Relational Approach' in J Liu, M Travers and L Change (eds) *Comparative Criminology in Asia*. Berne. Springer. 17–32

Looney, A (2015) *Vladimir Jankélévitch: The Time of Forgiveness*. New York. Fordham University Press

MacCulloch, D (2003) *Reformation: Europe's House Divided 1490–1700*. London. Penguin Books

MacIntyre, A (1990) *Three Rival Versions of Moral Enquiry*. London. Duckworth

Mackenzie, A (2005) 'The Problem of the Attractor: A Singular Generality between Sciences and Social Theory', *Theory, Culture & Society* 22(5): 45–65

Manguel, A (2018) *Packing My Library* https://www.bbc.co.uk/programmes/b09xjb68

Mantzovinos, C (2016) 'Hermeneutics', https://stanford.library.sydney.edu.au/archives/spr2017/entries/hermeneutics/

Marion, JL (2002a) *Being Given: Toward a Phenomenology of Giveness*. Stanford. Stanford University Press

Marion, JL (2002b) *Prolegomena to Charity*. New York. Fordham University Press

Marion, JL (2012) *God Without Being*. Chicago. University of Chicago Press

Marshall, C (2021) 'Sin, Shame and Atonement: A Challenge for Secular Redemption' in A Millie (ed) *Criminology and Public Theology: On Hope, Mercy and Restoration*. Bristol. Bristol University Press. 111–44

Martin, D (2014) *Religion and Power: No Logos without Mythos*. Farnham. Ashgate

Martinson, R (1974) 'What works? Questions and answers about prison reform', *The Public Interest* 35: 22

Maruna, S (2001) *Making Good: How Ex-Convicts Reform and Rebuild Their Lives*. Washington. American Psychological Association.

Maruna, S, Matravers, A and King, A (2004) 'Disowning Our Shadow: A Psychoanalytic Approach to Understanding Punitive Public Attitudes', *Deviant Behavior* 25: 277–99

Mason, A (2020) *Fifty spiritual homilies of St Macarius the Egyptian*. New York. Alpha Editions

Massumi, B (1996) *A User's Guide to Capitalism and Schizophrenia. Deviations for Deleuze and Guattari*. Cambridge. MIT Press

Mauss, M (1977) *The Form and Reason for Exchange in Archaic Societies*. London. Routledge

McBride, J (2014) 'Christ Existing as Concrete Community Today', *Theology Today* 7(1): 92–105

McBride, J and Fabisiak, T (2020) 'Bonhoeffer's Critique of Morality: A Theological Resource for Dismantling Mass Incarceration' in L Hale and W Hall (eds) *Dietrich Bonhoeffer: Theology and Political Resistance*. Maryland. Lexington Books. 89–110

McCarthy, C (2005) *No Country for Old Men*. New York. Knopf

McEvoy, K and Mika, H (2002) 'Restorative Justice and the Critique of Informalism in Northern Ireland', *The British Journal of Criminology* 42(3): 534–62

McKeever, M (2017) *One Man, One God: The Peace Ministry of Fr Alec Reid C.Ss.R*. Dublin. Redemptorist Publications

Merleau-Ponty, M (1968) *The Visible and the Invisible*. Evanston. North Eastern University Press

Milbank, J (2006) *Theology and Social Theory: Beyond Secular Reason*. 2nd edn. Oxford. Blackwell

Miller, J (1993) *The Passion of Michel Foucault*. London. Flamingo

Miller, W (1990) 'Carnivals of Atrocity: Foucault, Nietzsche, Cruelty', *Political Theory* 18(3): 470–91

Miller, W and Rollnick, S (2002) *Motivational Interviewing*. 2nd edn. New York. Guilford Press

Millie, A (2016) *Philosophical Criminology*. Bristol. Policy Press

Milovanovic, D (2014) *Quantum Holographic Criminology: Paradigm Shift in Criminology, Law and Transformative Justice*. Durham. Carolina Academic Press

Milovanovic, D (2019) *Postmodern Criminology*. London. Routledge

Ministry of Justice (2021) Government to introduce 'Harper's Law' Press release, https://www.gov.uk/government/news/government-to-introduce-harper-s-law

Minow, M, Ryan, M and Sarat, A (eds) (1995) *Narrative, Violence and the Law: The Essays of Robert Cover*. Michigan. Michigan University Press

Mitchell, A and Trawney, P (eds) (2017) *Heidegger's Black Notebooks: Responses to Anti-Semitism*. New York. Columbia University Press

Moore, JF (1927) *Judaism in the First Centuries of the Christian Era: The Age of the Tannaim*. Cambridge, MA. Harvard University Press

Moore, M (2010) 'Meditations on the Face in the Middle Ages (with Levinas and Picard)', *Literature and Theology* 24(1): 19–37

Nancy, JL (2000) *Being Singular Plural*. Stanford. Stanford University Press

Nash, M (2016) ' "Scum Cuddlers": Police Offender Managers and the Sex Offenders' Register in England and Wales', *Policing and Society* 26(4): 411–27

Nash, M and Williams, A (eds) (2008) *The Anatomy of Serious Further Offending*. Oxford. Oxford University Press

Nelson, M. (1991) 'Utilitarian Eschatology', *American Philosophical Quarterly* 28(4): 339–47

Nietzsche, F (2003) *Thus Spoke Zarathustra*. St Ives. Penguin Books

Nixey, K (2017) *The Darkening Age: The Christian Destruction of the Classical World*. London. Macmillan

Notopolous, J (1938) 'Mnemosyne in Oral Literature', *Transactions and Proceedings of the American Philological Association, 1938* 69: 465–93

O'Connell, P (2017) '*Enargeia*, Persuasion, and the Vividness Effect in Athenian Forensic Oratory', *Advances in the History of Rhetoric*, 20(3): 225–51

Osakabe, Y (2016) 'Restoring Restorative Justice: Beyond the Theology of Reconciliation and Forgiveness', *International Journal of Public Theology* 10(2): 247–71

Oughorlian, JM (2012) *Psychopolitics: Conversations with Trevor Cribben Merrill*. East Lansing. Michigan University Press

Palmer, T (2007) *The Symphony of Sorrowful Songs*. DVD. Voice Print Records

Panganiban, A (2020) 'Theology of Resilience Amidst Vulnerability in the Book of Ruth', *Feminist Theology* 28(2): 182–97

Pauling, J (2021) 'Don't Immanentize the Eschaton: Against Right-Wing Gnosticism', *The Public Discourse*, https://www.thepublicdiscourse.com/2021/02/73937/

Peck, R (2016) *I Am Not Your Negro*. Arte films.

Pepinsky, H (2006) *Peacemaking: Reflections of a Radical Criminologist*. Ottawa. University of Ottawa Press

Pepinksy, H (2013) 'Peacemaking Criminology', *Critical Criminology* 21: 319–39

Pepinsky, HE and Quinney, R (Eds.). (1991) *Criminology as Peacemaking*. Bloomington. Indiana University Press.

Picard, M (2015) *The Flight from God*. South Bend. St Augustine's Press

Plato (2003) *The Republic*. London. Penguin Books

Polizzi, D and Draper, M (2013) 'The Therapeutic Encounter Within the Event of Forensic Psychotherapy: A Phenomenological Hermeneutic of Givenness of the Other Within the Therapeutic Relationship', *International Journal of Offender Therapy and Comparative Criminology* 57(6): 720–35

Porter, J (2005) *Nature as Reason: A Thomistic Theory of the Natural Law*. Cambridge. Eerdmans

Prigogine, I and Lefever, R (1973) 'Theory of Dissipative Structures' in H. Haken (ed) *Synergetics: Cooperative Phenomena in Multi-Component Systems*. Wiesbaden. Springer Fachmedien. 124–35

Pycroft, A (2010) *Understanding and Working with Substance Misusers*. London. Sage

Pycroft, A (2014) 'Probation Practice and Creativity in England and Wales: A complex systems analysis' in A. Pycroft and C. Bartollas (eds) *Applying Complexity Theory: Whole Systems Approaches to Criminal Justice and Social Work*. Bristol. Policy Press. 199–220

Pycroft, A (2018) 'Consciousness in Rather Than of: Advancing Modest Claims for the Development of Phenomenologically Informed Approaches to Complexity Theory', *Journal of Theoretical and Philosophical Criminology* 10: 1–20

Pycroft, A (2019) 'From a Trained Incapacity to Professional Resistance in Criminal Justice' in A Pycroft and D Gough (eds) *Multi-Agency Working in Criminal Justice: Theory, Policy and Practice*. 2nd edn. Bristol. Policy Press. 25–40

Pycroft, A (2020) 'Between Athens and Jerusalem in Peacemaking Criminology: The Importance of Weak and Marginal Positions', *Journal of Theoretical & Philosophical Criminology* 12: 188–99

Pycroft, A (2021a) 'St Paul among the Criminologists' in A Millie (ed) *Public Theology and Criminology: On Justice, Mercy and Forgiveness*. Bristol. Bristol University Press. 71–91

Pycroft, A (2021b) 'The Surveillance of Substance Misuse and the Drug Use Industry' in B Arrigo and B Sellers (eds) *The Pre-Crime Society: Crime, Culture and Control in the Ultramodern Age*. Bristol. Bristol University Press

Pycroft, A and Bartollas, C (eds) (2014) *Applying Complexity Theory: Whole Systems Approaches to Criminal Justice and Social Work*. Bristol. Policy Press

Pycroft, A and Bartollas, C (2018) 'Forgiveness as Potentiality in Criminal Justice', *Critical Criminology* 26: 233–49

Pycroft, A, Wallis, A, Bigg, J and Webster, J (2015) 'Participation, Engagement and Change: A Study of the Experiences of Service Users of the Unified Adolescent Team', *British Journal of Social Work* 45: 422–39

Pylkkänen, P (2015) *Mind, Matter and the Implicate Order*. New York. Springer

Rambo, S (2015) 'Refiguring Wounds in the Afterlife (of Trauma)' in R Kearney and B Treanor (eds) *Carnal Hermeneutics*. New York. Fordham University Press. 263–78

Rayner, J (2020) 'Last Meals on Death Row, a Peculiarly American Fascination', https://www.nytimes.com/2020/03/10/dining/death-row-last-meals-jay-rayner.html

Richardson, W (1980) 'Phenomenology and Psychoanalysis', *Journal of Phenomenological Psychology* 11(2): 1–20

Ricoeur, P (2004) *Memory, History, Forgetting*. London. University of Chicago Press

Roberts, T. with Windle, J. (2015). *Forgiven: The Amish School Shooting, a Mother's Love, and a Story of Remarkable Grace*. Bloomington. Bethany House

Rohlf, M (2016) 'Immanuel Kant', https://plato.stanford.edu/entries/kant/

Ronel, N and Ben Yair, Y (2018) 'Spiritual Criminology: The Case of Jewish Criminology', *International Journal of Offender Therapy and Comparative Criminology* 62(7): 2081–102

Rosenberg, R (2018) 'Incarnate Meaning and Mimetic Desire: Saints and the Desire for God', in *The Givenness of Desire: Concrete Subjectivity and the Natural Desire to See God*, Toronto. University of Toronto Press. 139–56

Runions, E (2021) 'Carceral Sacrificonomics in the Time of Pandemic', *Critical Research on Religion* 9(1): 98–102

Sartre, JP (nd) *Being and Nothing-ness*. New York. Philosophical Library

Sartre, JP (1976) *Critique of Dialectical Reason*. London. NLB

Schama, S (2013) *The Story of the Jews: Finding the Words 1000 BCE-1492 BCE*. London. The Bodley Head

Schwager, R (2000) *Must there be Scapegoats? Violence and Redemption in the Bible*. Leominster. Gracewing

Scruton, R (2003) *A Short History of Modern Philosophy*. London. Routledge

Shakespeare, W (1975) *Hamlet*. London. William Collins & Sons

Shearing, C (1989) 'Decriminalizing Criminology: Reflections on the Literal and Tropological Meaning of the Term', *Canadian Journal of Criminology* 31(2): 169–78

Sheenan, T (2017) 'Martin Heidegger, "Nur noch ein Gott kann uns retten," Der Spiegel 30 (Mai, 1976): 193–219. Trans. by W. Richardson as "Only a God Can Save Us"' in *Heidegger: The Man and the Thinker*. Abingdon. Routledge. 45–67

Shestov, L (2016) *Athens & Jerusalem*. Athens. Ohio University Press

Siedentop, L (2015) *Inventing the Individual: The Origins of Western Liberalism*. St Ives. Penguin Books

Simmons, W (1999) 'The Third: Levinas' Theoretical Move from Anarchical Ethics to the Realm of Justice and Politics', *Philosophy and Social Criticism* 25(6): 83–104

Singh, D (2018) *Divine Currency: The Theological Power of Money in the West*. Stanford. Stanford University Press

Singh, D (2021) 'Economic Theology and Critique: A Response', *Critical Research on Religion* 9(1): 103–6

Skotnicki, A (2021) 'Persecuting the Prophets: Inequality, Insanity and Incarceration' in A Millie (ed) *Criminology and Public Theology: On Hope, Mercy and Restoration*. Bristol. Bristol University Press. 247–72

Smith, D and Protevi, J (2008) 'Gilles Deleuze', https://plato.stanford.edu/entries/deleuze/

Staal, R (2008) 'The Forgotten Story of Postmodernity', *First Things*, December: 35–8

Stokes, R (2014) 'Yhwh's Executioner', *Journal of Biblical Literature* 133(2): 251–70

Taylor, C (1989) *Sources of the Self: The Making of Modern Identity*. Cambridge. Cambridge University Press

The New Jerusalem Bible: Standard Edition (1985). London. Darton, Longman and Todd

Tillich, P (1971) *The Courage to Be*. London. Collins/Fontana

Tillich, P (1997) *Systematic Theology Volume One*. London. SCM Press

Tugwell, S (1979) *The Way of the Preacher*. London. Darton, Longman and Todd.

Underhill, E. (1960) *Mysticism*. London. Methuen and Co.

Van Wormer, K and Starks, S (2012) 'Therapeutic Jurisprudence, Drugs Courts and Mental Health Courts: The US Experience' in A Pycroft and S Clift (eds) *Risk and Rehabilitation: Management and Treatment of Substance Misuse and Mental Health Problems in the Criminal Justice System*. Bristol. Policy Press. 153–74

Vattimo, G and Zabala, S (2011) *Hermeneutic Communism: From Heidegger to Marx*. New York. Columbia University Press

Verdeja, E (2004) 'Derrida and the Impossibility of Forgiveness', *Contemporary Political Theory* 3: 23–47

Vincellete, A (1998) 'Introduction' in Pierre Rousselot, *The Problem of Love in the Middle Ages: A Historical Contribution*. Milwaukee. Marquette University Press

Vincent, G, Perrault, R, Drawbridge, D, Landry, G and Grisso, T (2021) 'Risk-Need-Responsivity Meets Mental Health: Implementation Challenges in Probation Case Planning', *Criminal Justice and Behavior* 48(9): 1187–207

Voegelin, E (2004) *Science, Politics and Gnosticism*. Wilmington. ISI Books

Von Balthasar, H (1990) *Mysterium Paschale: The Mystery of Easter*. San Fransisco. Ignatius Press

Von Kellenbach, K (2013) *the Mark of Cain: Guilt and Denial in the Post-War Lives of Nazi Perpetrators*. Oxford. Oxford University Press

Voss, D (2013) 'The Philosophical Concepts of Meat and Flesh: Deleuze and Merleau-Ponty', *Parrhesia* 18: 113–24

Wainhouse, A and Seaver, R (1990) *The Marquis de Sade: One Hundred and Twenty Days of Sodom*. London. Arrow Books

Walklate, S and Hopkins, A (2019) 'Real Lives and Lost Lives: Making Sense of "Locked in" Responses to Intimate Partner Homicide', *Asian Journal of Criminology* 14: 129–43

Wall, J (2001) 'The Economy of Gift: Paul Ricouer's Significance for Theological Ethics', *The Journal of Religious Ethics* 29(2): 235–60

Washington, J (ed) (1986) *A Testament of Hope: The Essential Writings of Martin Luther King Jr.* New York. Harper and Row

Ward, T and Maruna, S (2007) *Rehabilitation*. Abingdon. Routledge

Watkins, C (2011) 'The Real Relationship in Psychotherapy Supervision', *American Journal of Psychotherapy* 65(2): 99–116

Waugh, E (1964) *Brideshead Revisited*. London. Penguin Books

Webb, E (1988) *Philosophers of Consciousness*. Seattle. University of Washington Press

Wernick, A (1982 'De Sade and the Dead End of Rationalism', *Canadian Journal of Political and Social Theory / Revue Canadienne de theorie politique et sociale* 6(1–2)

Whitehead, P (2018) *Demonising the Other: The Criminalisation of Morality*. Bristol. Policy Press

Whitehead, P and Crawshaw, P (2013) 'Shaking the Foundations: On the Moral Economy of Criminal Justice', *The British Journal of Criminology* 53(4): 588–604

Whitmarsh, T (2017) 'Book review of The Darkening Age: The Christian Destruction of the Classical World by Catherine Nixey', *The Guardian*, 30 December

Williams, T and Bengtsson, J (2018) 'Personalism', https://plato.stanford.edu/entries/personalism/

Williams, WC (1962) *Pictures from Brueghel and Other Poems*. New York. Golden Eagle Press

Wilson, R (1983) 'Gnosticism' in A Richardson and J Bowden (eds) *A New Dictionary of Christian Theology*. London. SCM Press. 226–30

Yalom, I (2021) *The Theory and Practice of Group Psychotherapy (6th ed)*. New York. Basic Books

Yee, A, Zubovic, E, Yu, J, Shuddhaded, RM, Hildebrandt, S, Seidelman, W et al (2019) 'Ethical Considerations in the Use of Pernkopf's Atlas of Anatomy: A Surgical Case Study', *Surgery* 165: 860–7

Yoder, K (2020) 'Instruments of Immolation: Giorgio Agamben and the Eucharistic Reformations of the Sixteenth Century', *Critical Research on Religion*, https://doi.org/10.1177/2050303220952877

Young, J (2012) *The Criminological Imagination*. Cambridge. Polity

Zeitlin, S (1941) 'The Crucifixion of Jesus Re-examined', *The Jewish Quarterly Review* 31(4): 327–69

Žižek, S (2003) *The Puppet and the Dwarf: The Perverse Core of Christianity*. Cambridge, MA. Massachusetts Institute of Technology Press

Žižek, S (2009a) *The Parallax View*. Cambridge, MA. Massachusetts Institute of Technology Press

Žižek, S (2009b) *Violence*. London. Profile Books

Žižek, S (2011) 'The Fear of Four Words: A Modest Plea for the Hegelian Reading of Christianity' in C Davis (ed) *The Monstrosity of Christ: Paradox or Dialectic*. Cambridge, MA. Massachusetts Institute of Technology Press. 24–109

Index

References to figures appear in *italic* type;
those in **bold** type refer to tables. References to endnotes show the
page and chapter number and the note number (231ch2n3).